Government by referendum

MANCHESTER
1824

Manchester University Press

POCKET POLITICS

SERIES EDITOR: BILL JONES

Pocket politics presents short, pithy summaries of complex topics on socio-political issues both in Britain and overseas. Academically sound, accessible and aimed at the interested general reader, the series will address a subject range including political ideas, economics, society, the machinery of government and international issues. Unusually, perhaps, authors are encouraged, should they choose, to offer their own conclusions rather than strive for mere academic objectivity. The series will provide stimulating intellectual access to the problems of the modern world in a user-friendly format.

Previously published
The Trump revolt   Edward Ashbee
Lobbying: An appraisal   Wyn Grant
Power in modern Russia: Strategy and mobilisation   Andrew Monaghan
Reform of the House of Lords   Philip Norton

Government by referendum

Matt Qvortrup

Manchester University Press

The right of Matt Qvortrup to be identified as the author of this work has been asserted by him in accordance with the Copyright, Designs and Patents Act 1988.

Published by Manchester University Press
Altrincham Street, Manchester M1 7JA

www.manchesteruniversitypress.co.uk

British Library Cataloguing-in-Publication Data
A catalogue record for this book is available from the British Library

ISBN   978 1 5261 3003 7   paperback

First published 2018

The publisher has no responsibility for the persistence or accuracy of URLs for any external or third-party internet websites referred to in this book, and does not guarantee that any content on such websites is, or will remain, accurate or appropriate.

Typeset by
Servis Filmsetting Ltd, Stockport, Cheshire
Printed in Great Britain by
CPI Group (UK) Ltd, Croydon, CR0 4YY

Mr. Alan Clark (Kensington and Chelsea): On a point of order, Madam Speaker. I am most grateful for your allowing me to raise a point of order that relates to the language in which we communicate in this Chamber. Your predecessor once rebuked me for using the language of the Common Market: I said 'faute de mieux', for which he immediately called me to order. The word 'referendum' is being scattered about, but, although my hon. Friend the Member for Lichfield (Mr. Fabricant) used the correct plural, I have often heard colleagues refer to 'referendums', which is an exceedingly ugly term. May we have from you, Madam Speaker, a ruling, or at least an expression of preference, as to whether we continue to use the Latin word, which many would think historically appropriate in the Chamber, or whether you have no objection to the continual Anglicisation of the term and the use of the word 'referendums'? Were you to express a preference for the Latin form, which I hope you will, you would certainly be striking a blow for classical revivalism.

Madam Speaker: The right hon. Gentleman raises an esoteric point, albeit hardly a point of order: more a matter of taste. I notice that, in the public Bills list, the word 'referendums' is used in relation to Scotland and Wales. The word 'referendum' was first used in English 150 years ago, according to the Oxford English dictionary, which I have just consulted, and I imagine that, after 150 years, the House is now used to it. The plural is a matter of taste, but I have always preferred the use of the English language to any Latin form; I hope that that provides some guidance.

From *Hansard*, 3 June 1998, col. 282

Contents

List of figures and tables

Figures

Tables

Acknowledgements

The author wishes to thank Laurence Morel, Marc Plattner, Vernon Bogdanor, David Altman, Matthew Shugart, Mogens Hansen, Laurence Whitehead, Philippe Schmitter, Yanina Welp, Guy Lachapelle, Thomas Webster, Bill Jones, Tony Mason and Arend Lijphart for critical discussions in the process of writing this book. The author is especially grateful to Sebastian Qvortrup, BA (Hons), for critical proofreading and suggestions.

London, 10 August 2017

Introduction

'REFERENDUMS', wrote a columnist in *The Observer* in July 2016, 'are the nuclear weapons of democracy. In parliamentary systems they are redundant. Seeking a simplistic binary yes/no answer to complex questions, they succumb to emotion and run amok. Their destructive aftermath lasts for generations' (Keegan 2016: 43). It is a fair bet that the author did not vote for Brexit. The issue here is not to claim that politicians and pundits are fickle and unprincipled. The question here is an empirical one; was the pundit correct?

Are there more referendums now than in the past? And, if so, has that made the world become more democratic? Could it be that referendums are linked with the growth in social movements in recent years and the tendency to use alternative channels to challenge the status quo (see Della Porta 2006)? Or, conversely, is the undeniable prominence of referendums undermining representative democracy, as some (Topaloff 2017) have suggested? Or is the growing number of referendums just an indication of a weaker political class prone to miscalculations, as others (Glencross 2016) have suggested?

All these questions are addressed in the following pages. However, the process did not quite follow the plan initially expected or planned. That is in the nature of things.

The chapters in this short book were originally intended to form part of a coherent and theoretical whole; to show how the use of the referendum followed a strict, almost Hegelian pattern of the 'unfolding of freedom' throughout the ages – as the

German idealist philosopher might have put it. Yet the more I looked at the particular cases – especially the referendums in the United Kingdom held during the governments of Harold Wilson (1974–76) and David Cameron (2010–16) – the more it became clear to me that there were different, sometimes competing, patterns. Rather than following G.W.F. Hegel, I came to a conclusion much like the one Ludwig Wittgenstein reached when he wrote his *Philosophical Investigations*. As this book is written in the same spirit of this much more illustrious work, I feel justified in quoting the Austrian philosopher at length:

> After several unsuccessful attempts to weld my results together into such a whole, I realized that I should never succeed. The best that I could write would never be more than philosophical remarks; my thoughts were soon crippled if I tried to force them on in any single direction against their natural inclination. – And this was, of course, connected with the very nature of the investigation. For this compels us to travel over a wide field of thought crisscross in every direction. – The philosophical remarks in this book are, as it were, a number of sketches of landscapes which were made in the course of these long and involved journeys. The same or almost the same points were always being approached afresh from different directions, and new sketches made. Very many of these were badly drawn or uncharacteristic, marked by all the defects of a weak draughtsman. And when they were rejected a number of tolerable ones were left, which now had to be arranged and sometimes cut down, so that if you looked at them you could get a picture of the landscape. Thus this book is really only an album. (Wittgenstein 1953: vii)

This book, then, is a series of 'remarks' and 'sketches', which together form a mosaic rather than a coherent whole.

In the first chapter the world history of the referendum is outlined. A chapter follows this on the British experience up to 2010. This was initially intended to be a short overview of the previous referendums – and a detailed analysis of more recent votes. However, when researching the book I noticed that the referendum on European Economic Community (EEC) membership in 1975 (in effect the first Brexit referendum) in important respects mirrored the vote in 2017 – and yet in other ways was completely different. This, I felt, was important, and I consequently filled rather more pages on the 1975 vote. Thus this referendum looms large in Chapter 2, though we also consider the alternative vote referendum in 2011 and the referendum on Scottish independence in 2014.

Chapter 3 pertains to the United Kingdom European Union (EU) membership referendum in 2016, especially the campaign leading up to it. As in the previous chapter, this vote is analysed empirically but with several excursuses into the political theory.

After the analysis of the Brexit referendum, Chapter 4 reverts to the wide world and summarises some of the trends and tendencies in the use of the referendum internationally. As this overview suggests, Britain is not a unique case in holding referendums. The chapter shows that, notwithstanding the general assumptions about referendums, these are not usually associated with demagogues and populism, but the referendum has tended to be used as a constitutional safeguard. However, in Britain, a country without a formal written constitution, these safeguards were not in place. Consequently, a leader like David Cameron was able to use the referendum for party-political purposes in a way that arguably was detrimental to the political system. For the referendum to work – for this institution to be a constitutional safeguard – it must be a people's shield and not the government's sword.

1

The world history of referendums

Introduction

IN this chapter I trace the history of the referendum from its earliest origins to its present-day use – or, some would say, abuse. After a *tour d'horizon* of the earlier use of the direct democracy, it first presents a historical overview of the use of referendums from the Renaissance through to the First World War. It is pointed out that the referendum – contrary to assertions by Tuck (2016) – can be traced back to the fifteenth century. Despite the term's earlier use, the referendum began to be used in earnest only in the nineteenth century, when the Italian Risorgimento and the early years of the Swiss Federation (after 1848) essentially owed their existence to the use of the referendum. Having analysed these cases I take a closer look at the discussion about the referendum in the United Kingdom and the European continent. Drawing on a functionalist-inspired model, the chapter ends with reflections and research on why there has been an apparent increase in the use of the referendum since the 1980s.

The earlier history of direct democracy

Like so many other things political, the referendum in the form we know it today (a vote by the mass population on a policy proposal) was the invention of the French revolutionaries. The so-called Girondins – who were in conflict with the more radical Jacobins – proposed that the people should be allowed to veto constitutional changes. And this, according to Tuck, 'was the first time that the modern notion of a plebiscite or a referendum had been raised' (Tuck 2016: 143). It perhaps says a lot about the cavalier fashion in which direct democracy is treated that the otherwise well-informed scholar got it wrong. For, as we shall show below, the referendum had already operated for hundreds of years at this time. By the time of the French Revolution, the term *referendum* had first been used in what was to become present-day Switzerland, where, in 1684, the *Bürger* (all male citizens over the age of sixteen) were given the right to cast their votes on the policy issues that were submitted to them *ad referendum* by the elected representatives (Pieth 1958: 146).

But the Swiss were not the only ones to submit issues to the people, though they were the first ones to use the word *referendum*. Before we return to the use of direct democracy in modernity (the period after AD 1500), it is instructive to go back to the very beginning: to Greece and Rome.

As historians of ancient democracy can testify, direct democracy was the central element of the political system of ancient Greece, where in the fourth century BC decrees 'were passed by majority vote of those Athenians attending the meetings of the Assembly (*ekklesia*), which were held four times per civil month, or forty times per annum'. This system of direct democratic involvement was also characteristic of the Athenian democracy after the Peloponnesian War, i.e. between 400 and 320 BC (Hansen 1991).

It is possible to argue that the Romans employed a certain kind of direct democracy before the fall of the Republic in 49 BC. And, there are some suggestions that other peoples used what we today may describe as direct democracy. The Roman historian Tacitus (56–117) described the use of proto-referendums among Germanic tribes where 'on matters of minor importance only the chiefs debate; [but] on the major matters the whole community' (Tacitus 1970: 110). Similar stories could be told about the Italian Renaissance states. Niccoló Machiavelli eulogised a system of politics that had been brought into being 'by the consent of a whole people' – *da uno commune consenseo d'una universalità* (Machiavelli, III, 7). But it was not until the early sixteenth century that the institution was established in anything resembling the present-day referendum.

The referendum 1527–1789

Historically referendums were about self-determination. The first instances of referendums in anything like the present form date back to 1527 when the French King Francis I (1494–1547) held a plebiscite in Burgundy on whether to transfer the area to the Spanish King in 1527 as he had agreed to in the Treaty of Madrid (Vattel 1758: 263).

The people rejected the transfer and stayed with France. And scholars have later speculated (Wambaugh 1933: xxiii) – though without much by way of concrete evidence – that the French King was inspired by the Dutch philosopher Erasmus of Rotterdam (1466–1536) who in 1517 had made a case for the view that 'what power and sovereignty so ever you have, you have it by the consent of the people' (Erasmus 1907: 51).

Of course, 'the people' in those days comprised a rather small number: those entitled to vote were only property-owning males. Whether a practical man like King Francis devoured texts by Renaissance theologians – as suggested by Wambaugh (1933: xxiv) – can be questioned. However, a few years later, Francis's son, Henry II (1519–59) organised a plebiscite in 1552 in Verdun, Toul and Metz before their annexation (Solière 1901: 26).

Before the plebiscite, Bishop de Lénoncourt is reported to have said to the inhabitants of Verdun 'that the King of France had come as a liberator who will treat the citizens as good Frenchmen ... He appealed to the vote of the people' (Solière 1901: 26). It is noteworthy that the cleric used words such as *bourgeois* and *peuple* at a time when Jean Bodin (1530–96) expounded his theory of divinely sanctioned absolutism by the grace of God in *Six livres de la République* in 1579 (Bodin 1986).

But we have few contemporary accounts of what motivated

the use of referendums at the time. Indeed, it was almost a century before these practices were placed on anything like a theoretical footing. Hugo Grotius (1583–1645), the great legal scholar and father of international law, observed in *De Jure Belli ac Pacis* that 'in the alienation of a part of sovereignty, it is required that the part which is alienated consent to the act' (Grotius 2005: 570).

The referendum 1789–1920

The French Revolution heralded a new era of democracy. Rather predictably, therefore, referendums were embraced by the new rulers in Paris. Indeed, no less a theoretician than Baron de Condorcet (1743–94) had published a pamphlet in 1789 with the telling title *Sur la Nécessité de faire Ratifier la Constitution par les Citoyens* – roughly translated, 'in the necessity of the people ratifying the constitution' (Condorcet 1847).

At this stage this was not mere idle talk. Indeed, France's annexation of Avignon in 1791 took effect only after a referendum had been held in the area. A contemporary report read:

> Considering that the majority of the communes and citizens have expressed freely and solemnly their wish for a union with Avignon and France ... the National Assembly declares that in conformity with the freely expressed wish of the majority ... of these two countries to be incorporated into France. (cited in Martens 1801: 401)

It is conventional to note that the Congress of Vienna dealt a blow to the doctrine of self-determination – and, as a consequence, to the use of referendums: 'The Congress of Vienna in 1815 did not accept self-determination as a basis for reshaping the map of Europe' (Griffiths 2003: 38). The victors in the Napoleonic wars were conservatives who wanted to return to a time when the popular sovereignty was *not* the gold standard of political legitimacy. The perception was that the excesses of ideological fervour and the horrors of the Napoleonic wars gave democracy a bad name. This changed after the revolutionary year of 1848 when the referendum once again became fashionable, though only for Bonapartists: neither Republicans nor Monarchists liked it, and the Socialists abandoned it in this period.

Napoleon III, who used dubious plebiscites to claim popular legitimacy, especially espoused referendums. And in international affairs, self-determination of the people was accepted once again (Weitz 2008). Two areas are of particular interest. Italy – where several referendums were held in the name of self-determination as a part of the process to unify the country – and Schleswig-Holstein (between present-day Denmark and Germany), where a referendum was proposed, but not held, over the fate of the province.

The Risorgimento referendums in Italy were held to put pressure on the great powers that were reluctant to change the status quo. In a series of votes held between 1848 and 1870, different parts of Italy voted to join the new unified state under the constitutional monarch Victor Emmanuel of Sardinia. Camillo Benso di Cavour (1810–61) expressed the consensus among those advocating the use of referendums at the time in a letter before the referendum in Tuscany and Emilia in 1860:

> I await with anxiety the result of the count, which is taking place in Central Italy. If, as I hope, this last proof is decisive (*questa ultima prova*), we have written a marvellous page in the history of Italy. Even should Prussia and Russia contest the legal value of universal suffrage, they cannot place in doubt (*non potranno mettere in dubbio*) the immense importance of the event today brought to pass. Dukes, archdukes and grand-dukes will be buried forever beneath the heap of votes deposited in urns of voting places of Tuscany and Emilia. (Cavour 1883, vol. 3: 211, my translation)

Cavour was perhaps correct in expressing doubt about the sincerity of the commitment on the part of more autocratic powers such as Prussia and Russia, yet even these countries were surprisingly positive towards referendums on self-determination in the 1850s and 1860s.

Britain's mediation between Denmark and Prussia following the first part of the First Schleswig War in 1848–51 is a case in point. Lord Palmerston (the British foreign secretary 1846–51) suggested to Christian von Bunsen, the Prussian ambassador in London, that the dispute should be decided 'with reference to the ascertainable facts', and that these could be found only through a referendum (Palmerston 1848: 1321). The Prussian diplomat responded:

> Germany [sic!] cannot give up the principle declared on all occasions that no separation of any part of Schleswig can ever be thought of, unless the population in the northern districts themselves declare, by an open and unbiased manifestation of their intention to that effect. (Graf von Bunsen to Palmerston, 24 June 1848, *British and Foreign State Papers*, vol. 40: 1321)

The proposal was, however, rejected by the Danes, who militarily had the upper hand. In 1864, during an armistice following Prussian victories in the first part of the Second Schleswegian War, the Prussian foreign minister Peter Graf von Bernsdorff maintained at the London Conference that he was guided by the conviction that the 'conference should be aware of the wish of the people whose future they were debating [and that] the inhabitants of Schleswig should be consulted on the subject' (Bernsdorff, in *Conference of London*, Protocol No. 10, 1864).

The Danes rejected the proposal, believing – wrongly as it turned out – that the British would oppose Prussian annexation. After the Prussian defeat of Denmark, the Treaty of Prague made annexation conditional upon the consent of the people. However, in January 1867, Prussia (having realised opposition against its rule) annexed Schleswig-Holstein *in toto* without a referendum. Once again pragmatism – or *Realpolitik?* – triumphed over idealism.

The referendum on self-determination played a very minor role in the years following the Franco-German War. Tellingly, given that the referendum is often used in an opportunistic way, leading German lawyers now rejected the use of referendums whereas French international lawyers and intellectuals rediscovered the attractions of letting the people decide.

The referendum in Switzerland in the nineteenth century

Meanwhile the referendum was gaining prominence in Switzerland, and not just in the rather arcane form of *Landesgemeinde* (public open-air meetings where male citizens voted on local laws). That only men were allowed to vote was not unusual in those days. It is worth pointing out, though, that Swiss women gained the vote only in the early 1970s, all previous attempts having been vetoed in referendums.

Notwithstanding this deplorable and sexist discrimination, the Swiss pioneered the referendum and invented the term itself in the seventeenth century. Yet, although the device could be traced back hundreds of years, the modern use of the referendum was a result of a compromise that emerged in the period after the *Sonderbund War* (1848).

The Radical Party (from 1894 renamed and most commonly known as the Freisinnig-Demokratische Partei der Schweiz, FDP) was the dominant force in Swiss politics immediately after the civil war. The party pursued a twin track of muscular secularism and free-market and laissez-faire liberalism. Under the majoritarian (first-past-the-post) electoral system the party was able to win a majority of the seats in the Bundesrat (the executive) without winning a majority of the votes.

Realising that the Radical majority in the Bundesrat did not always have the support of the voters at large, and that Catholics and Protestants shared some of the same interests, their confessional disagreements notwithstanding, the confessional groups began to push for the introduction of a popular veto: a referendum in which the voters could vote on legislation already passed (provided they could collect a specified number of signatures). The Radicals, for their part, wanted to strengthen their stranglehold on power. After a constitutional reform was rejected in 1872, the Radicals accepted that the popular referendum should be introduced in return for federal control over legislation (something the Catholics opposed). It was not anticipated that the referendum would be widely used as it would require collaboration between Catholics and Protestants against the secular Radicals.

But – contrary to the Radicals' predictions – the confessional groups were able to co-operate despite their theological disagreements. This resulted in a number of important changes that challenged the Radicals' virtual monopoly on legislative power in the period before the First World War. The rejection of a law on the establishment of a federal ministry of education in 1884 (the very thing the Radicals had sought), the introduction of the Constitutional initiative in 1891 and the rejection of a more liberal temperance law in 1903, are all examples of how non-liberal groups prevented radical legislation. Through the referendum, parties in opposition were able to shape public policy. In the view of one observer, 'strong political minorities were able to threaten and mobilize for an activation of the optional referendum, until they were eventually co-opted into the government' (Serdült 2017: 85). This tendency became stronger after Switzerland became a multi-party system. But Switzerland is *sui generis*; a special case of direct democracy: in the local vernacular, a *Sonderfall*.

Referendum after the First World War

In the wake of the First World War – at the behest of the American President Woodrow Wilson – eight referendums were held to determine the borders in Europe. Wilson's commitment to self-determination was not – it seems – only a result of a study of the European doctrines espoused in the wake of the French Revolution, still less of the ideals of the Italian Risorgimento or the doctrines of Grotius and other philosophers. Rather, Wilson's commitment was also inspired by his early years as a populism campaigner for more direct democracy. Earlier in his career, Wilson had stated his commitment to direct democracy in domestic politics. He had noted that,

> It must be remembered that we are contrasting the operation of ... the referendum, not with representative government, which we possess in theory ... but with the actual state of affairs, with legislative processes which are carried out in secret, responding to subsidized machines, and carried through by men whose happiness it is to realize that they are not their own masters but puppets of the game. (quoted in Munro 1912: 87)

These ideals – so it seems – inspired the president in his espousal of national self-determination. Wilson did not – as commonly assumed – mention referendums in his famous Fourteen Points speech to Congress on 8 January 1918. However, it is clear from the context that the twenty-eighth president wanted the decisions regarding the borders to be taken through plebiscites by the peoples concerned. As Wilson noted:

> Peoples may now be dominated and governed only by their own consent. Self-determination is not a mere phrase. It is an imperative principle of action, which statesmen will henceforth ignore at their peril. The settlement of every question, whether of territory, of sovereignty, of economic arrangement, or of political relationship [must be] upon the basis of the free acceptance of that settlement by the people immediately concerned, and not upon the basis of the material interest or advantage of any other nation which may desire a different settlement for the sake of its own exterior influence or mastery. (Wilson quoted in Farley 1986: 3)

For all his idealism Wilson was not always true to his word. Indeed, a referendum organised by the council in Tyrol was ignored – at the insistence of the French – despite the fact that more than 90 per cent voted for union with Germany. Not all the votes resolved matters. Yet, it is worth noting that 'It was precisely in the those [sic] areas where plebiscites were refused (with the exception of Alsace-Lorraine) – Danzig, the Polish corridor and the Sudetenland – that were the subject of revisionist claims by the Nazis in the 1930s' (Bogdanor 1981b: 145).

Tellingly, German revisionist claims were not made in areas that were ceded after a referendum, such as Nord Schleswig where there was a large German-speaking minority. This is possibly because 'frontiers that were fixed by plebiscite could not easily be undermined' (Bogdanor 1981b: 145).

Elsewhere, the use of the referendum took on somewhat different forms. In the United States so-called Populists proposed and ensured the adoption of initiatives (referendums on laws proposed by the people) and referendums (votes on laws enacted by the legislature). In continental Europe the referendum eventually degenerated into abuse by Hitler and other dictators, and in the United Kingdom the referendum was much theorised and little used (this is covered in the next chapter).

From the 1870s, the debate about the introduction of mechanisms of direct democracy had played a considerable role in German politics. In *Das Gothaer Programm* from 1875 – the Social Democrat Party's (SPD's) manifesto that was famously criticised by Karl Marx in his *Critique of Gotha Programme* (Marx 2000) – the party had demanded 'direct law making by the people', something Marx had dismissed as 'nothing beyond the old democratic litany familiar to all' (Marx 2000: 611). This demand was repeated in the *Erfurt* Programme in 1891 in which the party demanded direct legislation through the people through the power of proposing and rejecting Bills. This commitment was shared by social democratic and radical parties in Europe. Indeed, all the socialist parties in countries bordering Germany adopted the idea of referendums (Bullock and Reynolds 1987). However, this enthusiasm among practitioners was in sharp contrast to the misgivings that existed among intellectuals in Germany at the time – including socialists. Karl Kautsky (1854–1938), arguably the SPD's leading theoretician, warned in the 1890s that the referendum would be abused by the government (Kautsky 1893), and later complained that 'the referendum violated the principle that all laws ought to be a result of compromises between different groups' (Kautsky 1911: 78). However, the concept of the referendum was included in the

Weimar constitution – mainly at the instigation of the sociologist Max Weber (Weber 1958: 468).

Between the First and Second World Wars, the inclusion of the referendum in the German constitution inspired far-right thinkers and became a vehicle for a kind of plebiscitary authoritarianism. In Germany, the involvement of the people was to be limited to plebiscites. Although this is often overlooked in the literature (though see Berbera and Morrone 2003: 24), Carl Schmitt (1888–1985), a political theorist who joined the Nazi Party, advocated the use of the plebiscite as a mechanism of conferring legitimacy upon decisions by autocratic rulers.

Schmitt recognised that in the present day no one 'would remain on the throne against the will of the people' (Schmitt 1988: 29). However, due to its divided nature and opposing political parties, a parliamentary system could not speak for 'the people'. As a result of this 'institutions of direct democracy' would always be 'in a position superior to the so-called indirect democracy of the parliamentary state' (Schmitt 1988: 60). But the voters were not in a position to pose the questions: 'the people can only respond yes or no. They cannot advise, deliberate and discuss' (Schmitt 1988: 93). Hence, 'plebiscitary legitimacy requires a government or some other authoritarian organ in which one will have confidence that it will pose the correct question' (Schmitt 1988: 90). Schmitt's theory was adopted by the National Socialists, who submitted issues to the voters in order to acquire the 'plebiscitary of a decision through one will' (Schmitt 1988: 92).

The practical use of referendums after 1945

'The use of referendums around the world has proliferated remarkably in the past 30 years' (Tierney 2012: 1). This growing use of mechanisms of direct democracy is not only characteristic of politics at the national level. Votes on devolution in Denmark (Greenland), Britain (Scotland, Wales and Northern Ireland) and Spain (Galicia, the Basque Country, Andalusia and Catalonia) are prominent examples at the sub-national level (Qvortrup 2014).

Why was it that after 1980 people began to demand referendums? Is this an indication that the world has become more democratic? Why is it that political parties have apparently been willing to concede to these demands and to relinquish their monopoly on legislating?

It is noteworthy that there were very few referendums in and around the 1960s. To be sure, the Swedes voted on three pension plans in 1957 and on whether to drive on the right in 1955. And in France General Charles de Gaulle used the referendum in a somewhat plebiscitary fashion to win approval for the introduction of the Fifth Republic (1958), withdrawal from Algeria (1961) and the direct election of the Executive (1962) And he duly resigned when he failed to win a referendum on Senate reform in 1969. But these were the exceptions. So too, were the Danish, Irish and Norwegian referendums on EEC (now EU) membership in 1972.

It all began to change in approximately 1980. In the 1980s, several referendums were held on 'new' issues. The Swedes and the Austrians voted on nuclear power in 1979 and 1980, respectively, and there was a sense that the referendum was being used to resolve issues that cut across traditional political cleavages. The political parties had failed to represent the electors as well as they had done before.

Referendums became a 'legitimization tool for constitutional changes that occasionally serve as a synchronization mechanism between politicians and citizens' (Altman 2011: 197). The same explanation held at the municipal level where local referendums contributed 'an additional qualitative dimension to the public space of local politics by opening new channels for public deliberations on issues' (Schiller 2011: 69).

To understand the apparent change towards a greater use of direct democracy some historical context might be useful. In the middle of the twentieth century, political theorists were sceptical of the people. 'How', asked B.R. Berelson and his colleagues, 'could a mass democracy work at all if all the people were deeply involved in politics?' (Berelson 1954: 318). Their answer was that it could not and that referendums were a bad idea. This view prevailed in the 1960s during the behavioural phase. (The behavioural phase was an era in the history of political science when scholars and students of politics consciously sought to use insights from the behavioural sciences, above all sociology and psychology. The 'phase' ended in the early 1970s.) During this period political scientists took a dim view of the voters' knowledge about politics. And it was the general consensus that 'the effective operation of a democratic political system usually requires some measure of apathy and non involvement' lest the voters should become overstretched (Huntington 1975). As a prominent observer opined,

> [Democracy does] not mean and cannot mean that the people actually rule in any obvious sense of the terms 'people' and 'rule.' Democracy means only that the people have the opportunity of accepting or refusing the men [!] who are to rule them. But since they might decide this also in entirely undemocratic ways, we have had to narrow our definition by adding a further criterion identifying the democratic method, viz., free competition among would-be leaders for the vote of the electorate. (Schumpeter 1942: 242)

Forty years on, the view had changed. Countries that had held few or no referendums (such as the Netherlands, Luxembourg and Iceland) began to submit issues to referendums. And, while no nationwide referendums had been held in Germany since the 1930s, practically all the *Länder* (States) made provisions for referendums – sometimes even votes initiated by the citizens themselves (Schiller 2011) – after the German unification in 1990.

How can this be interpreted theoretically? From a theoretical point of view referendums can provide a democratic safety valve and a mechanism for letting out political steam. According to the input–output model (Almond et al. 2006), the political system is one in which groups in the surrounding environment *articulate* demands, which are channelled into the *Political System* by *aggregators* and transformed into policies, decisions and actions, in other words *outputs*.

In the original model, the function of articulators was carried out by civic groups and trades unions (Almond et al. 2006: 67), and the role of aggregators was performed by political parties, which 'aggregated' the views 'articulated' by organisations and civic groups (Almond et al. 2006: 81). By performing this function, the political parties ensured that concerns and demands from the environment were translated into policies.

The referendum could thus be seen as a consequence of a malfunction on the input side of the political system. If political parties do not respond to demands articulated by the groups outside the political system, this can be resolved by using an alternative aggregator – namely the referendum – and, if we want to go a step further, by citizens' initiatives, which allow citizens to initiate legislation rather than merely vote on proposals initiated by the elites.

This analysis is supported historically. In the period from 1920 to 1970, when the West European party system was 'frozen' along the lines of the main social, economic and religious cleavages (see Rokkan and Lipset 1967), there were very few referendums, as the political parties were both able and willing to respond to views articulated by the interest groups they represented.

Referendums began to be used and demanded virtually at the same time as *dealignment* – i.e. at the time when the relationship between 'aggregators' and 'articulators' broke down; at the time when the frozen party system began to thaw; at the time when the number of party-identifiers began to drop. As Altman observes, referendums are 'used twice as frequently today compared with fifty years ago and almost four times more than at the turn of the twentieth century' (Altman 2011: 65).

This cannot be proved categorically, but it could be speculated that the people felt that political parties were not willing and able to represent them. The views articulated by minority groups (especially on the 'New Left') failed to be aggregated by political parties, and at the same time voters on the centre right felt that the traditional centre-right parties were unresponsive to views of the New Right.

Of course, the voters were still broadly in agreement with the dominant political parties. Sören Holmberg, writing about Scandinavia, for example found that there was congruence between voters' preferences and the policy positions of the representatives in 79 per cent of cases (Holmberg 2000: 155). But there was disagreement in the remaining 21 per cent. It is arguable that it was to cater for the latter kind of incongruence that the referendum became a convenient alternative – an 'aggregator'. This analysis is not only plausible in Western Europe and other developed nations; it is also corroborated by research in younger democracies, for example in Latin America. According to Altman:

> Because institutionalized party systems may ... become overinstitutionalized, they have serious dilemmas for channeling social demands, they lack the required flexibility to do so, and ultimately they will be subject to massive demands for movement towards citizens' preferences. (Altman 2011: 197)

But social science is contextual rather than universal. The use of the referendum and other forms of direct democracy as an alternative aggregator might also explain the growing use of mechanisms in the United States, where the initiative and the referendum were used to spearhead the 'Reagan revolution'. (The so-called 'Prop 13.' in California is a famous example of how the 'people' bypassed a recalcitrant political elite to demand tax cuts.)

But the story is a different one in the former Communist countries and in authoritarian regimes in Latin America. But, on closer inspection, this too conforms to the pattern. In the absence of established political parties, a mechanism was needed to confer legitimacy upon the newly enacted constitutions in former autocratic regimes (whether Communist or not); thus the referendums after the fall of dictatorships in Spain and Brazil – and in Russia, Hungary and practically all other former Communist countries – are examples of how the referendum was used as an alternative 'aggregator'. Once party systems were established in these countries, the number of referendums

dropped slightly. Functionalism may not be in fashion in theoretical journals but the model still accounts for developments
in the real world. (Functionalism was the idea that the political
system could be studied as if it were a biological system. As
different parts of the body have separate 'functions', so have
different institutions different roles to play in the 'body politick'.)

To relieve the political system from demands, referendums
(and other forms of direct democracy) have served 'as institu-
tionalized, sporadic safety valves of political pressure' (Altman
2011: 198). By developing mechanisms for(letting out political
steam in the form of referendums,)the political systems seem
to have become more legitimate. And, it appears – though hard
evidence is difficult to come by – that countries with more referendums have suffered lower levels of political distrust in the
political elites: 'giving people more voice is widely considered
a promising remedy against the current crisis of democracy'
(Bernard 2012: 199).

2

The history of the referendum in Britain

THE reader will note that Britain was largely absent from the previous chapter. While there were referendums from the 1970s and onwards in the United Kingdom, the UK was not in the forefront of the development of the device – at least not as far as its practical use was concerned. But the absence of actual experience does not mean that the British political elite were oblivious to the possibilities of involving the people.

It was the constitutional theorist Albert Venn Dicey (1835–1922) who first put forward a political theory of the referendum. But he was not the first one to consider the idea that the people could be asked to make decisions on major policy matters. As far back as the Putney Debates (1647), radicals had without success urged the introduction of the referendum. In a series of articles and papers, including in the sixth edition of his influential treatise *An Introduction to the Study of the Law of the Constitution* and in the article 'Ought the Referendum to be Introduced into England?' (Dicey 1981), he made a case for the referendum as an alternative second chamber; a mechanism through which the 'prerogatives of the crown' could be turned into 'the privileges of the people' (Dicey 1890: 503).

Alarmed about W.E. Gladstone's intention to introduce Home Rule for Ireland without having campaigned for this in a general election, Dicey wanted to introduce a check on the elected government at a time when the House of Lords had lost its position as a veto-player. Dicey stressed that the referendum was 'the one available check on party leaders [and the only institution that could] give formal acknowledgement of the doctrine which lies at the basis of English democracy – that a law depends at bottom for its enactment on the consent of the nation as represented by its electors' (Dicey 1911: 189–90).

At the time these ideas were well received by prominent Conservative politicians. The Conservative Prime Minister Arthur Balfour (1848–1930) positively eulogised the referendum as a brake on change. The 'referendum [is] ... used ... always in a Conservative sense', and this device was his 'idea of Tory Democracy' (quoted in Bogdanor 1981a: 9). In the light of this, it was not surprising that the Conservative and Unionist Party pledged in its manifesto in 1910 that it would hold a referendum before introducing tariff reform (a tax on imported goods from outside the British Empire). However, the Conservatives failed to win the election in January 1910, and the promise was dropped by Balfour's successor Bonar Law (Bogdanor 1981a: 24).

The referendum was mainly an institution championed by British Conservatives. However, some on the moderate left were also endorsing the idea too. In his influential book *Liberalism* the social liberal L.T. Hobhouse (1864–1929) admitted that 'there are many issues for which it is ill suited' (Hobhouse 1994: 89), but he found it 'regrettable that so many liberals have closed the door on the referendum' (Hobhouse 1994: 89). A prominent left-leaning Liberal who had not 'closed the door' but who actively endorsed the referendum was J.A. Hobson (1858–1940). Hobson – whose critical work on imperialism inspired Lenin's *Capitalism, the Highest Stage of Capitalism* (Lenin 1948) – had made a case for the referendum as a mechanism for breaking the deadlock between the House of Commons and the House of Lords. This argument was pertinent to the crisis that emerged in 1909, the year when the book was published. After Lloyd George, the Liberal chancellor of the exchequer, had proposed a budget including progressive taxation and benefits for the poor and elderly (the so-called People's Budget), the Conservatives used their majority in the House of Lords to block it (Murray 1973). One of Hobson's arguments in *The Crisis of Liberalism* was that such deadlocks could be resolved by reference to the people instead of through a general election. In his own words:

> The formal legislative power left to the new Second Chamber should be the power of causing a Bill of the Commons which they disapprove to be submitted to a separate vote of the electorate, in order to test the question whether or not the people desires that the disputed Bill should become law. (Hobson 1909: 32)

However, nothing came of this suggestion.

The Labour Party took a different approach. It was opposed to the referendum. This is somewhat remarkable as its sister parties on the European continent, above all the German SPD (see previous chapter), were enthusiastic about direct legislation by the people. This was not a peripheral issue. Rather, prominent members of the Labour movement spoke against the device. No less a politician than Ramsay MacDonald (who later became Labour's first prime minister in 1924) rejected the referendum, and described it as 'but a clumsy and ineffective weapon which the reaction can always use more effectively than democracy, because it, being the power to say "No" is far more useful to the few than to the many' (MacDonald 1911: 153).

After the Constitutional crisis of 1910/11 the referendum largely disappeared from the political discourse – though the Conservative Lord Curzon unsuccessfully suggested a referendum to halt the introduction of female suffrage (Pugh 2000: 165).

In 1930, in the shadow of the Depression, the issue of tariff reform again surfaced. The newspaper proprietors Lord Rothermere, the owner of the *Daily Mail*, and Max Aitken, the owner of the *Daily Express* (he was later ennobled as Lord Beaverbrook), threatened to establish a new party on the right if Stanley Baldwin, the Tory leader, did not commit the Conservatives to the policy. The prospect of the United Empire Party fielding as many as fifty candidates in the next general election forced Baldwin to take action. Mindful that many in the party were opposed to the populist policy advocated by the two proprietors, but equally aware of the damage the new party could do to the Tories, Baldwin (somewhat like David Cameron over eighty years later, see Chapter 4) embraced the referendum. Rather than opposing tariff reform, the leader of the Opposition promised that a referendum would be held on the issue in the event of a Conservative victory. Under the heading *This is Baldwin's Pledge to You*, the Conservative Central Office issued *Circular No. 3155*, which stated 'There will be no food taxes at the General Election and no food taxes ever without a direct vote by the people' (Goodhart 1971: 45). This satisfied their Lordships. The United Empire Party did not contest the election. After the election the Labour leader Ramsay MacDonald continued as prime minister in a National government (with Conservative, Liberal and National Labour members) and the referendum pledge made by the Conservative leader was forgotten. Once again, the institution slipped into oblivion.

For the next almost thirty years no serious proposal for referendums were advanced. Though, it should not be forgotten that, in 1945 Winston Churchill – who had vigorously opposed the referendum as a Liberal Home Secretary in 1911 (Bogdanor 1981a: 28) – proposed that a referendum be held on whether the wartime coalition should continue until the end of the Japanese War. However, Clement Attlee wrote to Churchill, and flatly rejected his proposal:

> I could not consent to the introduction into our national life of a device so alien to all our traditions as the referendum, which has only too often been the instrument of Nazism and Fascism. Hitler's practices in the field of referenda and plebiscites can hardly have endeared these expedients to the British heart. (Attlee quoted in Bogdanor 1981a: 35)

That Hitler had used (rigged and stage-managed) referendums did not mean that all referendums are dubious. As Philip Goodhart, a Tory MP, observed some years later in response to Attlee's denunciation of referendums:

> Hitler's use of the referendum to further totalitarian ends provides no more proof that referenda help would-be

> dictators than Stalin's use of the Supreme Soviet to support
> his cult of personality discredits parliamentary democracy.
> Both a referendum and a representative assembly can be
> twisted by an unscrupulous leader. (Goodhart 1971: 80)

And, of course, Attlee's refusal was not based on political philosophy, let alone on a careful study of continental constitutional practices at a time when referendums were used extensively by very credible democratic governments. But the argument worked. That is in the nature of political rhetoric: principles, arguments and seemingly erudite references to foreign constitutional practices are used to pursue political ends.

All this was literally academic at the time. The referendum was not seriously debated until the end of the 1960s. The change in constitutional doctrine happened as a result of the schism over membership of the EEC.

Referendums in the 1970s

It was not until 1973 that the first major referendum was finally held in Britain, with previous attempts limited to local polls, such as that on temperance in Wales.

After the outbreak of hostilities in Northern Ireland, the Conservative Prime Minister Edward Heath decided to submit the future of the province to a verdict by the people. Voters in the province were asked, 'Do you want Northern Ireland to remain part of the United Kingdom?' The Catholic minority boycotted the referendum; thus the outcome was not reflective of the will of the people. On a 58 per cent turnout 98 per cent voted to remain part of the United Kingdom. The referendum merely cemented the demographic realities, and arguably prompted the more radical among the nationalist or Catholic minority to resort to violence and terror. Not for the first time blunt majoritarianism led to strife and exacerbated the conflict. But the Border Poll received little coverage, particularly compared to the following major referendum in 1975.

In the light of more recent history, it is thus instructive to look at the referendum on EEC membership that took place in the mid-1970s. Not because history repeats itself, but rather to show that it does not, and – perhaps – to warn subsequent generations not to believe complacently that the past is a guide to the present.

History lessons from the 1975 referendum?

To understand why the referendum came to the fore in the early and mid-1970s requires us to look at the whole political ecology at the time. The referendum was not merely a result of one specific development. It was not caused by a single event, rather it emerged as a result of an interplay of different factors; 'In sum' ... 'history is not a chain of independent events' (Steinmo 2008: 128).

The idea of a more-or-less united Europe was the brainchild of Sir Winston Churchill, who in a speech in 1946 suggested that a partnership should be established among European countries as a 'Kind of United States of Europe' (Churchill 1946). However, Churchill did not entertain the possibility that Britain could join the European Communities. Consequently, when the other European countries courted Britain in the 1950s, the answer was unenthusiastic. This was the position until Harold Macmillan became prime minister in 1957. Macmillan applied for membership of the EEC in 1961. His application was resolutely dealt with by France: president Charles de Gaulle rejected British membership in 1963. Undeterred, Macmillan's successor but one, Harold Wilson, sent a second application of membership in May 1967. Six months later, de Gaulle once again vetoed the application.

Everything changed in 1969. After the failure to win a referendum on a reform of the Senate and the introduction of regional government, de Gaulle resigned and was replaced by Georges Pompidou (Hayward 1969). The latter did not share his predecessor's visceral dislike for all things British and said he was content for Britain to join – though he wanted to hold a referendum first.

While there had been no referendums during the Troisième République (1870–1940), the tradition of holding referendums was revived after the Second World War, and used extensively after Charles de Gaulle became the first president of the Fifth Republic in 1958. Referendums on the new constitution (1958), on the secession of Algeria (1961 and 1962) and on the direct election of the president (1962) turned France into a kind of plebiscitary democracy in which the president often sought to bypass a recalcitrant legislature by going straight to the people.

To ensure that the president represented the people, de Gaulle introduced what he described as 'the referendum system' (de Gaulle 1971: 7). This, de Gaulle wrote, would enable the president to submit to a referendum any government proposal pertaining to the country's institutions. In the event of a grave crisis 'he [the president] should be able to be empowered to take the measures demanded by the circumstances' (de Gaulle 1971: 7) by securing the support of the voters in a referendum.

The situation was very different in the United Kingdom. Here all talk about the referendum was, at best, a distraction. When the issue of British membership of the EEC began to be discussed, both Labour and Conservative MPs were concerned about the constitutional implication of Britain joining an organisation that could override the will of a majority of the MPs and peers at Westminster. At Prime Minister's Question Time on 14 July 1966, the possibility of a referendum was raised by John Lee, MP. The Labour backbencher was a colourful character, who held rather unusual views. (He once suggested to a political scientist that the defence forces should be replaced by a group of assassins trained to hunt down dictators and eliminate them – I owe this story to Bill Jones, the Series Editor, who interviewed Lee in 1969.) That Lee could be fairly described as a loose cannon perhaps explained the Prime Minister's curt response. Asked by Lee if the prime minister would 'introduce legislation to provide for the use of the referendum as part of British constitutional practice', Wilson promptly responded with a monosyllabic 'No'.

Unsatisfied with the answer, Lee asked:

> Is my right hon. friend aware that in the happily very unlikely event of this country being in a position to enter the Common Market, no machinery exists to enable the British people to end what Hugh Gaitskell called a thousand years of British history?

Once again, Wilson was clear:

> The tradition for a considerable part of that thousand years is that decisions of great moment of this kind have to be taken by the elected Government of the day, responsible to this House. The constitutional position is that whatever this House decides in such a matter, or any other matter, is the right decision. (House of Commons Debates, 14 July 1966)

At this stage British membership of the EEC was, as John Lee had put it, a 'very unlikely event'. But, as noted, this changed after the resignation of de Gaulle and the more positive mood music coming out of Paris. The issue of British membership was a distinct possibility, indeed a likely one. By the end of 1969 it seemed only a matter of time before Britain would become a member of what was often referred to as 'the Common Market'. And once again, this prompted questions from those opposed to joining. The Labour backbencher Keith Campbell was one. He argued, very credibly, that a referendum was needed as the prevailing system of representative government failed in the case of the EEC issue. Those of the voters who did not share the major parties' desire to join the Common Market had no way of expressing their reservations, as no party that represented their position. A few months before the election Campbell proposed a Ten-Minute Rule Bill that would

> 'Allow the electors of Great Britain and Northern Ireland the right to decide by way of referendum whether Great Britain should enter the European Economic Community.' I submit that legislation of this kind is necessary because without it the people of Britain, who have never been consulted on this important issue, will never be consulted. The three major political parties have all declared themselves

> to be in favour of this country joining the Common Market.
> It therefore follows that this question will never be an elec-
> tion issue and the people will have absolutely no chance
> of ever being able to express their views on it through
> the ballot box at a General Election. (House of Commons
> Debates, 10 December 1969)

Such theoretically sound arguments of political theory did not
cut any ice with the political leaders of any of the parties. The
very idea of holding a referendum was still anathema to the
politicians of all the major parties. During the 1970 election,
the incumbent Prime Minister Harold Wilson was still adamant
in his opposition to any referendum – and so were the other party
leaders, the Conservative Edward 'Ted' Heath and the Liberal
leader Jeremy Thorpe. Indeed, in the television programme
BBC Election Forum, the latter even said, 'One of the principles
of democracy – and people may not like it, they may not like
democracy – is that you elect members of Parliament to use their
own judgement' (quoted in Butler and Kitzinger 1976: 11).

There was no disagreement between the Prime Minister and
the leader of the Liberal Party. Harold Wilson was equally cate-
gorical in his denunciation of the referendum. Asked if he would
contemplate a vote on membership of the EEC, Wilson was blunt
and unequivocal: 'the answer to that is "No" ... The answer is I
shall not change my mind on that' (quoted in Goodhart 1971: 17).

But Wilson lost the election in 1970 (the Conservatives won
a majority of 31 seats). Losing an election to an opponent few
Labour politicians rated was a blow and it is surprising that
Wilson survived as Labour leader. At this precarious time it was
important for him to appear as a unifying figure, especially as
the Labour Party was evenly split on the merits of membership
of the EEC. Many of the backbenchers – and the then powerful
unions – made it very clear to Wilson that they were less than
enthused by the prospect of joining the Common Market.

It may be difficult to understand why Wilson's rejection
of a referendum suddenly changed and why his very public
and unambiguous denunciation of the referendum changed.
Wilson's conversion to the referendum did not happen over-

night and must be understood in the context of both political and economic changes and challenges at the time. There is often a danger of focusing too narrowly on superficial similarities between political epochs. Sometimes such comparisons are exaggerated to a degree that basic factors are overlooked in pursuit of that elusive general pattern which scholars cherish. It is easy to draw parallels between the travails of Harold Wilson in the 1970s and those of Conservative prime ministers like John Major twenty years later and David Cameron forty years later.

But in simply looking for a pattern, by simply assuming that history somehow repeats itself, we fail to acknowledge the way in which idiosyncratic developments played a role. And, above all, by narrowly focusing on signs of recurrent patterns, we fail to acknowledge how different the situation was in the early 1970s.

The negotiations over EEC membership did not happen in isolation. There were many interrelated factors that prompted the Labour Party to seek alternative policies to force what was considered to be a weak government to resign or call an election. Harold Wilson was a politician who – to put it kindly – was not overly burdened by doctrine, principle or commitment to cast-iron values. And the political developments offered him opportunities aplenty.

The Heath government was going through a rough patch. In January 1972 thirteen innocent civilians had been shot in Northern Ireland on what became known as 'Bloody Sunday'; the prime minister was locked in a struggle with coal miners; unemployment rose to nine hundred thousand. All these factors added to the pressure and the unpopularity of the government. There was a considerable chance – or risk – that Heath would be forced to resign. The reason was not least the disquiet about the European Communities Bill, which aimed to transfer all hitherto enacted European legislation into UK law, now only slowly moving through its various parliamentary stages. Many Tory MPs were defying the party whip and made it clear that they were willing to vote the government down even if this would result in a general election.

In this climate it was not surprising that Labour sought to find ways of defeating the government. Tony Benn, a left-wing member of the shadow cabinet and MP for Bristol (curiously in Burke's old constituency), had been an early advocate of referendums and a critic of the theory of pure representative democracy espoused by his distant predecessor (Benn, quoted in Butler and Kitzinger 1976: 12). Benn had already proposed a referendum at a Special Party Conference in July 1971, though this came to naught.

Benn realised that he was getting nowhere with idealistic arguments. He promptly changed tactic. He now simply proposed a referendum on EEC membership (Butler and Kitzinger 1976: 18–19) at a shadow cabinet meeting on 15 March 1972. Predictably, given his earlier opposition, Wilson spoke against the idea and Benn's proposal was defeated.

But then something changed. The following day President Pompidou announced that, instead of letting the French legislature vote on the EEC accession treaty, he would use the provision for an advisory referendum contained in the French constitution and ask the people. A week later Ted Heath was struggling to find a way out of the impasse in Northern Ireland. Having introduced direct rule in the six counties, William Whitelaw, the Secretary of State for Northern Ireland, proposed that regular referendums should be held to determine whether the citizens in Northern Ireland wanted to join the Republic of Ireland. All of a sudden referendums had become legitimised almost by default. If the French, and even the UK government itself, accepted that a plebiscite could be held to determine the complex question of Northern Ireland, surely the issue of EEC membership too should be submitted to the voters. Undeterred by his defeat in the shadow cabinet, Tony Benn – wearing his hat as Party Chairman (Butler and Butler 1994: 144–5) – once again proposed a referendum but this time he proposed it to the National Executive Committee, which backed it – and only two weeks after the Labour shadow cabinet had rejected the very idea of a referendum, it now endorsed one when it met on 29 March. Wilson himself was now in favour of a referendum.

The change of heart was not merely a result of the apparent

legitimacy of referendums. It was also a result of a new opportunity to defeat the government. Some Conservative MPs – most notably Enoch Powell – were determined to stop the transfer of powers to Brussels. Although Powell's commitment to referendums was at best skin-deep, he tabled an amendment to the European Communities Bill calling for a referendum. There was now a real chance that the Heath government could be defeated – provided that the Labour Party stayed united. But it didn't. Not all members of the shadow cabinet were as relaxed about constitutional principle as Harold Wilson. His deputy Roy Jenkins resigned and fired a parting shot against the idea of a referendum, 'By this means [a referendum]', said Jenkins, 'we would not have forged a more powerful continuing weapon against progressive legislation than anything we have known in this country since the curbing of the absolute powers of the House of Lords' (quoted in Butler and Kitzinger 1976: 19). That the Lords were an unelected body of aristocrats, and not the 'people' themselves, seemed of minor importance for the future Baron Jenkins of Hillhead.

The revolt against Wilson's *volte-face* saved the Heath government. While 209 Labour MPs supported the shadow cabinet's new position and voted for the amendment, 63 abstained – among them Roy Jenkins. The European Communities Bill was adopted by 284 votes to 235 on 18 April 1972. A week later, the French voters convincingly endorsed British membership of the EEC in a referendum (67 per cent voted '*oui*' (Leleu 1976)).

This could have been the end of the debate about the referendum had it not been for the hardening of Labour's position. Spurred on by trades unions, who saw the EEC as a capitalist plot, a resolution committed a future Labour government to 'negotiate':

> The reservation of the power of the British Parliament over its [the EEC's] legislation ... and to halt immediately the entry arrangements including all payments to the European Communities ... until such terms have been negotiated, and the assent of the British electorate has been sought. (The Labour Party 1972: 195)

These demands – perhaps much like the demands of Conservative backbenchers in 2015 – were politically unrealistic and legally dubious. Once Britain had become a member of the EEC on 1 January 1973 it had to accept the *Acquis communautaire,* the accumulated legislation, legal acts and court decisions which constituted the body of European law, including the fundamental principle that EEC law trumps legislation enacted by national parliaments. The requirement that Wilson, if re-elected, should 'negotiate' the 'reservation of the power' of the Westminster Parliament was a non-starter legally as well as politically. But, prudently, Wilson did not raise reservations.

Wilson's renegotiation of EEC membership

The issue of EEC membership did not feature much in the surprise election called by Edward Heath in February 1974. Issues such as the growing tensions in Northern Ireland, the quadrupling of oil prices (after the Yom Kippur War in 1973) and above all industrial relations were the most important. To be sure, those who carefully read the Labour Party Manifesto – *Let Us Work Together* – *Labour's Way Out of the Crisis* – would have noticed a boisterous section setting out Her Majesty's Loyal Opposition's commitment to a renegotiation of the British terms of entry to the European Communities. Wilson – who penned the manifesto – wrote that it was a 'profound political mistake' that the Heath government had accepted 'the terms of entry to the Common Market, and to take us in without the consent of the British people'. If re-elected, he pledged, 'a Labour Government will immediately seek a fundamental re negotiation of the terms of entry'. Further, the manifesto continued,

> The Government will be free to take decisions, subject to the authority of Parliament, in cases where decisions of the Common Market prejudge the negotiations. Thus, the right to decide the final issue of British entry into the Market will be restored to the British people. (Wilson 1974)

Even in the early 1970s it was acknowledged that Parliament had – legally speaking– transferred sovereignty to the European Communities, and as a result Westminster was no longer able to pass legislation in contravention of Community law. The pledge made by Labour was clearly in breach of Britain's treaty obligations as well as in clear contravention of the *Acquis communautaire.*

But this was politics – not law. And although the Labour Party acknowledged the legal position, setting out a tough position served a purpose. To understand why we need to look at how a referendum can be seen as a bargaining chip.

The referendum as a bargaining chip

When the Labour Party was elected on 28 February 1975, Wilson found it difficult to claim a mandate for anything. Labour had polled fewer votes than the Conservatives – the former won 37.1 per cent, the latter 37.9 per cent – but he won four more seats than the Conservatives, who finished with 297 MPs. With tacit support from the Liberals' fourteen members and an underhand understanding with the Scottish and Welsh nationalists, Harold Wilson was able to form a government (Butler and Kavanagh 1974). However, most observers at the time predicted, rightly, that Wilson would call another election. This was held in October 1974 and saw Labour returned with an overall majority of three.

Immediately after the election in February, the new foreign secretary, James Callaghan, continued to make demands which he must have realised at the time were unpalatable for Britain's new partners in the EEC. His speech to the Council of Ministers was, *The Financial Times* wrote, 'blunt to the point of rudeness' (2 April 1974) when he demanded that Britain be given concessions on the budget, overseas trade with former colonies and a host of issues pertaining to the Common Agricultural Policy (CAP).

Why did the new Labour government make such – seemingly – unrealistic demands? And why did the new government threaten a referendum? The tactic was far from unique, and has been used several times subsequently, but the British Labour government was the first to use the referendum as a bargaining chip, or what more theoretical political scientists call a two-level game (Topaloff 2017). As in the cases of Poland and Spain some decades later, the British government used the referendum to force the other countries to make concessions. In large measure, this worked – at least in the 1970s.

Initially, the other countries were not enthusiastic about the British demands, and the reactions from pundits and politicos who had helped Britain gain membership could, at best, be summed up as disappointed. Walter Scheel, the German foreign minister, said he 'could not accept that Britain was such a special case' and his French opposite number Michel Jobert pointed out that the original member states had paid a fair price to bring Britain into the community (Butler and Kitzinger 1976: 30–1). Yet the other countries were aware that failure to give at the very least token concessions to the British could lead to the embarrassing situation of the largest newcomer leaving the EEC. Further, many of the smaller nations (Denmark, Ireland, the Benelux countries) were keen to keep Britain in as a counterweight to what they saw as Franco-German dominance, and, on their part, the French wanted to keep Britain in as a counterbalance to an increasingly economically powerful Germany. And, lastly, the United States had made it clear that it preferred the United Kingdom to remain a member of the West European association of states.

The Labour government's gamble and the often harsh rhetoric – during the election campaign for the October election Wilson even described the EEC as 'a shambles' – paid off. At the summit in Dublin in the spring of 1975, the other members accepted a change to the budget rules demanded by the British as well as rules for preferential trade with former colonies (Butler and Kitzinger 1976: 40–1). But Callaghan did not repatriate British sovereignty; the outcome fell considerably short of what had been demanded in the Labour Party manifesto in February 1975.

Not surprisingly, many of the Labour politicians who had been sceptical about EEC membership – and who had expected Callaghan to get more concessions – were disappointed. 'The anti-marketers', as David Butler and Uwe Kitzinger wrote in their account of the referendum, 'could rightly claim that renegotiation had hardly been fundamental' (1976: 45). And yet, the referendum held a few months later resulted in a landslide success for Wilson. Unlike David Cameron almost forty years later, Wilson was able to 'frame' the debate (see Chapter 3).

The referendum campaign in 1975

The Wilson government was acutely aware that the referendum was a thorny issue, not least for the Labour Party. Many in the party, and indeed among its voters, were hostile to the Common Market. But Wilson and Callaghan gradually became enamoured of the EEC. In their meetings with colleagues from other countries they realised that their European colleagues were pragmatic and sensible, and that all the talk about 'ever closer Union' and other lofty expressions from the preamble of the Treaty of Rome was often mere talk. In a historical perspective it is, perhaps, remarkable how much this situation differs from that forty years later. Whereas David Cameron – and before him Tony Blair – was exasperated and impatient with Europe and fell out with colleagues (Seldon and Snowdon 2015: 168), Wilson and Callaghan warmed to Europe the more they dealt with their counterparts on the continent. Maybe the other leaders were more sympathetic towards Britain then, or maybe Wilson and Callaghan were just better politicians than Cameron and Blair.

But there were also historical idiosyncrasies at play: unique factors that favoured the position of the pro-marketers. Helmut Schmidt had replaced Willy Brandt as German chancellor and, like Callaghan, the new *Bundeskanzler* was a committed Atlanticist with a pragmatic attitude towards the EEC. In the autumn of 1974, Schmidt had even addressed the Labour Party conference, where he spoke in English, quoted Shakespeare and personally convinced Harold Wilson about the merits of staying in Europe on grounds of socialist solidarity (Butler and Kitzinger 1976: 37).

Not all Wilson's comrades were convinced, however. The Conference passed a motion by 3,007,000 to 2,949,000 votes calling for Britain to leave the EEC (Butler and Kitzinger 1976: 37). Not a large margin of victory but − more disturbingly − an indication that the Labour Party was almost evenly split on the matter. Acknowledging this split, Harold Wilson allowed his colleagues in the cabinet to differ on Europe. Collective responsibility, almost an article of faith in a system based on cabinet government, was abandoned for the first time since 1832. Even before the renegotiation had ended, Wilson said:

> The circumstances of this referendum are unique, and the issue to be decided is one on which strong views have long been held which cross party lines. The Cabinet has therefore decided that if, when time comes, there are members of the Government (including of the Cabinet) who do not feel able to accept and support the Government's recommendation, what ever it might be, they will, once the recommendation has been announced, be free to support and speak in favour of a different conclusion in the referendum campaign. (quoted in Buckley 2006: 76)

Wilson, again mindful of the split within Labour, did not leave it at that. The enabling legislation contained provisions for a financial grant to both sides (the so-called 'umbrella organisations') and these were given equal air time (Balsom 1996: 213). Further, careful consideration went into finding the right wording to the question. They settled for

> 'DO YOU THINK THAT THE UNITED KINGDOM SHOULD STAY IN THE EUROPEAN COMMUNITY (THE COMMON MARKET)?' (quoted in Butler and Kitzinger 1976: 61).

It is often believed that referendums, almost by default, result in a No vote. When the device was first debated in the late Victorian Age, this was one of the concerns raised. Henry Sumner Maine, a distinguished legal scholar, warned:

> It is possible, by agitation and exhortation, to produce in the mind of the average citizen a vague impression that he desires a particular change. But, when the agitation has settled down on the dregs, when the excitement has died away, when the subject has been threshed out, when the law is before him with all its detail, he is sure to find in it much that is likely to disturb his habits, his ideas, his prejudices, or his interests; and so, in the long-run, he votes 'No' to every proposal. (Maine 1976: 111)

On the basis of Maine's assumption, it was to be expected that the 1975 referendum would end in defeat for the government. And, on the basis of the earliest opinion polls, it looked as if Britain's membership was coming to an end less than two years after it had joined. In the first poll of the year, a Gallup Poll published in the *Daily Telegraph* on 24 January 1975, 33 per cent said they would vote to stay in the EEC; 41 per cent would vote to leave (Särlvik et al. 1976). The tide soon turned. Wilson, a wily campaigner, who won four of the five elections he contested (1964, 1966, February 1974 and October 1974), skilfully played on the unpopularity of the most prominent anti-marketers, the former Conservative minister Enoch Powell on the far right and the Labour left-winger Tony Benn. Of course, campaigning didn't do it alone. The Yes campaign outspent its opponents by a factor of an estimated 10 to 1. A month later, the Yes side (run by Britain in Europe) had pulled ahead and was leading by 8 per cent. In March the lead had grown to 16 per cent and in May the pro-marketers had a comfortable lead of 34 per cent (Butler and Kitzinger 1976: 250). On polling day (5 June 1975) 67.2 per cent voted for Britain to stay in Europe on a 64.5 per cent turnout (Balsom 1996: 213). The issue seemed to be settled. Neil Marten, one of the few Conservatives to vote for withdrawal (Butler and Kitzinger 1976: 52), said, 'We the anti-marketers, pressed for this referendum. We had it and we've got the result. And I think we've got to accept that that is the wish of the British people' (Butler and Kitzinger 1976: 274). Tony Benn was equally magnanimous in defeat:

> I have just been in receipt of a very big message from the British people. I read it loud and clear ... By an overwhelming majority the British people have voted to stay in and I am sure that everybody would want to accept that. That has been the principle of all of us who have advocated the referendum. (Bogdanor 1981a: 42)

Of course there were dissenting voices. Enoch Powell struck a pessimistic note and declared that the Yes vote meant that 'never again ... will an Englishman live for his country or die for his country; the country for which people live and die was obsolete and we have abolished it' (Enoch Powell, 1975, quoted in *The Daily Telegraph*, 9 July 1975).

Despite some misgivings about the campaign, and the Yes side's financial superiority, most of the voters viewed the referendum as a positive new development. According to a contemporary account, 'new personnel have been drawn into political local life, some of them already casting about for new causes in which to organize party co-operation ... certain bridges and some greater mutual understanding was built up across party barriers' (Bogdanor 1981a: 42).

The 1975 referendum was not the last one held under the Labour government. In the latter part of the government's life, opponents of the policy of establishing parliaments in Scotland and Wales forced the weak minority government into concessions. The first concession was that the proposed policy had to be submitted to a referendum. And, having won that, they further demanded – and won support for – a provision that stipulated that a Yes vote had to constitute 40 per cent of the eligible voters and not merely a majority of those voting.

In the 1979 referendums the proposal for a devolved assembly in Wales was rejected by a large margin of 4 to 1. In Scotland a majority voted for devolution, but, as this constituted only 32 per cent of the eligible voters, the proposal was defeated. Following the defeat, the Labour government lost a vote of no-confidence

Table 1   Referendums in the United Kingdom 1973–2014

Area	Question	Turnout (%)	Yes vote (%)	Year
Northern Ireland	Do you want Northern Ireland to remain part of the United Kingdom?	58.60	98.90	1973
United Kingdom	Do you think the United Kingdom should stay in the European Community (Common Market)?	65.00	67.20	1975
Scotland	Do you want the Provisions of the Scotland Act 1978 to be put into effect?	63.72	51.60	1979
Wales	Do you want the Provisions of the Wales Act 1978 to be put into effect?	79.00	20.60	1979
Scotland	I agree that there should be a Scottish Parliament	60.40	74.20	1997
Scotland	I agree that a Scottish Parliament should have tax-varying powers	60.40	63.40	1997
Wales	Do you agree that there should be a Welsh Assembly as proposed by the Government?	50.20	50.30	1997
London	Are you in favour of the Government's proposals for a Greater London Authority, made up of an elected mayor and a separately elected assembly?	34.60	72.00	1998

Table 1   (continued)

Area	Question	Turnout (%)	Yes vote (%)	Year
Northern Ireland	Do you support the Agreement reached at the multi-party talks on Northern Ireland and set out in Command Paper 3883?	81.10	71.10	1998
North East	Should there be an elected assembly for the North East region?	47.71	22.07	2004
Wales	Do you want the Assembly now to be able to make laws on all matters in the 20 subject areas it has powers for?	35.60	63.40	2011
United Kingdom	At present, the UK uses the 'first past the post' system to elect MPs to the House of Commons. Should the 'alternative vote' system be used instead?	42.20	32.00	2011
Scotland	Should Scotland be an independent country?	84.50	44.70	2014

Source: The Electoral Commission

in the House of Commons. The referendum had – at least indirectly – led to the fall of a government.

Whether it was for this reason or others, there were no referendums in the years of Conservative government under Margaret Thatcher (1979–90) and John Major (1990–97). This changed when Labour won the 1997 election.

After Tony Blair's New Labour government was elected, referendums, once again, became fashionable: votes on devolution for Scotland and Wales (1997), on whether to have an elected mayor in London (1998) and on the Good Friday Agreement in Northern Ireland (10 April 1998) were successful. However, in 2004 a referendum on a regional assembly in the North-East of England was overwhelmingly rejected by the voters (Knock 2006). These votes seemed to be the result of political opportunism rather than principle. None of the policies were controversial, and neither Blair himself nor any of his senior ministers seemed to be philosophically committed to referendums let alone to the more idealistic concerns regarding direct democracy.

Cameron's referendums 2010–14

'Great idea, I am all for that as you know.' David Cameron was 'very keen on referendums' – or so he said when he chatted to this author on the Eurostar on a trip back from Brussels in the spring of 2007. After his election as Conservative leader in 2005, he often waxed lyrical about the virtues of more citizen involvement. The youngish Conservative leader championed localism and an assortment of idealistic proposals for direct citizen engagement. He was soon to be tested. And, in many ways, he delivered – though perhaps not in the way he would have wanted.

Upon coming to power in 2010 the Conservative–Liberal Democrat coalition government held two referendums and presided over a third. In March 2011 a majority of the voters supported further devolution to Wales (the Welsh Assembly would henceforth be able to pass primary legislation). Later in the same year a referendum was held on whether to replace the first-past-the-post electoral system with the alternative vote (the proposal was rejected by a clear majority (Qvortrup 2012)). And finally, in 2014, 55 per cent of the Scottish voters voted No to the question *Should Scotland be an independent country?* (Cairney 2015).

The Welsh referendum was politically less interesting – although the formidable campaigner Rachel Banner almost singlehandedly challenged the elite consensus and was able to show that not all voters in Wales were enthusiastic about devolution (McAllister and Cole 2012). But all in all, this referendum was politically insignificant and did not have any lasting effect on the political debate in Britain.

The same was true for the referendums on the alternative vote in 2011. Of British voters 68.9 per cent rejected a proposal to change the electoral system from first-past-the-post to the alternative vote (AV). The turnout was 42 per cent. The referendum – as discussed extensively elsewhere (Qvortrup 2013) – was largely a referendum on the trustworthiness of the Liberal Democrat leader Nick Clegg. This was catastrophically low after his party had broken his campaign promise to abolish tuition fees only to increase them after his party joined in coalition with the Conservatives. The Conservatives (and many leading Labour politicians) were successful in running a campaign that focused on individuals and exaggerated claims. These were – as later admitted (Hodges 2011) – exaggerated. But the tactics worked.

The Scottish referendum

The Scottish referendum on 18 September 2014 was one of the most important polls in British history; it concerned the very existence of the nation. (We shall deal with an even more important one in the next chapter). The referendum had been a manifesto commitment when the Scottish National Party surprisingly won an outright majority in the Scottish Parliament in the election in 2011. (It was elected on the same day as the AV referendum.). Some of the unionist parties argued – with some justification – that a referendum was what lawyers call *ultra vires*. The Scottish government, its popular mandate notwithstanding, did not have a legal right to hold a referendum; under British law, citizens are free to do everything as long as it is not legally prohibited; public bodies, by contrast, are allowed only to do things

Table 2   Selected opinion polls: Scottish independence, 2014

Date	Yes	No	Don't know
25 Feb	38	55	7
12 May	34	46	20
6 Aug	37	50	13
2 Sept	47	45	8
10 Sept	49	42	9
16 Sept	45	49	6

Sources: Angus Reid, YouGov, ComRes, ICM

that are expressly provided for in law. As the Scottish Parliament is not explicitly allowed to hold a referendum, such a vote is – from a strictly legal point of view – outside its competence, in plain English, illegal. But the Scottish government – much like the government in Catalonia three years later – pressed on regardless.

This legal hiccup was resolved when David Cameron and the Scottish first minister Alex Salmond signed the Edinburgh Agreement in October 2012. The British prime minister – unlike his Spanish counterpart – was willing to gamble: in his case that the Scots would vote No but by a substantial margin. We shall return to that. The agreement allowed the Scots to hold a vote in September 2014. At this stage the opinion polls were still massively in favour of the status quo ante. Only about 30 per cent of Scottish voters were in favour of independence. From a political point of view, Cameron's acceptance of the SNP administration's demand seemed low-risk and gave him an air of magnanimity.

Throughout 2013 and in the early part of 2014 the polls began to narrow, though still with a clear majority in favour of No. In February 2013, the Yes vote stood at 32 per cent according to YouGov. It remained relatively static until the last month of the campaign when it rose to 40 per cent and sensationally, on 10 September, with only eight days to go, an ICM poll showed the Yes side had nudged ahead with a 49–42 per cent lead. In the last week of the campaign, following the intervention of Gordon Brown, No regained the lead.

What happened during the campaign? In the early spring of 2014 the British government issued a number of statements intended to show the consequences of independence. Backed up by his opposite number Ed Balls, the chancellor of the exchequer George Osborne suggested that Scotland would not be allowed to use the pound in the event of independence. And later the UK government issued calculations that purported to show that setting up a new administration would cost £1.5 billion (or one per cent of GNP).

Both of these interventions backfired. In the latter case the data was based on figures from Patrick Dunleavy, an independent-minded academic. However, the political scientist – who had not been consulted personally – said the figures had been misinterpreted and called them 'ludicrous' when interviewed on the BBC. Likewise, the suggestion that Scotland would not be allowed to share the pound or enter into a so-called currency union was rebuffed by SNP, which pointed out that the international practice is that the successor state is saddled with the debt after a breakup. Instead of stopping the slow move towards Yes, the government interventions arguably had the effects of spurring on the debate. Even the tabloids were full of discussions about policy issues, and at town hall meetings around the country, 'ordinary' voters were discussing the referendum and its implications.

The discussions seemed to favour the Yes side. With one week to go, the Prime Minister intervened and promised that in the event of a No vote far more powers would be transferred to Scotland. The former prime minister Gordon Brown reinforced this message on 8 September in a barnstorming speech in which he effectively promised devo-max before St Andrew's Day. This intervention stemmed the tide: the No campaign regained its lead and went on to win by a 10 per cent margin.

In the aftermath of the referendum it was universally acknowledged that the campaign had been tough but fair. More importantly still, the high turnout (84.6 per cent – the highest in UK history) proved that politics can fire people up. Unlike the 2011 referendum, the 2014 referendum led to a more engaged public as evidenced by the turnout in British referendum history and well above the paltry 65 per cent who voted in the 2010 general election. The Scottish referendum was a model to be emulated in other countries, not least because the two sides had sufficient time to present their case to the voters.

After the Scottish referendum there was a sense – on both sides – that the referendum had provided an opportunity for people to engage in civic engagement; as a kind of proof that Alexis de Tocqueville was right when he said, 'the most powerful and perhaps the only means of interesting men [and women] in the welfare of their own country is to make them partners in government' (Tocqueville 1961: 252). This enthusiasm was not to last.

Brexit campaign: the anatomy of a bitter divorce battle

POLITICAL science has often – especially in the United States – been characterised by reliance on statistical methods and reductionism that seeks to strip the analysis down to the barest essentials. There is a place for this kind of analysis, and indeed, it has been practised by this author (Qvortrup 2013). And yet quantitative analyses cannot stand alone. In fact, it is often observed that in seeking to reduce everything we may eliminate the very essence of what we are searching for. That is, there is a danger that we may 'bleach human behaviour of the very properties that interest us before we even begin to examine [them]' (Geertz 1973: 17). Inspired by this approach, this chapter takes a 'thick description' look at the Brexit referendum campaign.

The end of the campaign

It was rather unexpected. That, perhaps, was why David Cameron's voice broke ever so slightly when he announced his resignation in the morning of 24 June 2016. The night before, the Conservative Prime Minister had hosted an informal champagne party for friends in 10 Downing Street. The mood was optimistic, jubilant even. Campaigners were handing out stickers with the simple message *I'm In*; their Vote Leave counterparts were absent from the capital. If any of the assembled guests had cared to go to the countryside, indeed if they had ventured just two miles beyond the M25 London ring road, they would have seen a poster with the slightly xenophobic slogan *Halt ze German Advance – Vote Leave*.

Whether the gathered guests at Number 10 were in denial is an open question. To a degree they had reasons to be cautiously optimistic. The markets expected a Remain vote and the latest opinion polls showed a relatively solid lead. Indeed, Andrew Cooper (aka Baron Cooper of Windrush), the founder of the polling firm Populus and David Cameron's pollster, had predicted a 10 per cent win for Remain, according to one newspaper (*Sunday Times*, 26 June 2016, A1).

The buoyancy was further boosted when UKIP leader Nigel Farage apparently conceded defeat shortly after polls had closed at 10 pm. In an ill-tempered outburst – peppered by a quantum of sour grapes (and undoubtedly several pints of ale) – the Eurosceptic admitted to the BBC, 'I think Remain will edge it, yes. The massive increase in voter registration will be the reason for that.' The excuse that the extension of the voter registration could have swung the referendum was met with derision among those in the Remain camp; as proof, if such was needed, that Farage was a sore loser and as evidence that his commitment to democracy was skin-deep, opportunistic or non-existent.

All this was soon to change. After the first result from Gibraltar (a massive win), Sunderland declared for Leave and shortly thereafter Newcastle (long believed to be a bastion of Remain supporters) confirmed the trend. A very narrow win for Remain in the Tyneside capital showed only 50.7 per cent for Remain. Trouble was brewing. The guests left Cameron's party. He went to bed.

At 4 am the Prime Minister was woken up and told it was all over: that a majority of the British voters had voted to leave the European Union. Two hours later, the official result was declared. David Cameron's career was all over and had ended in ignominy and self-inflicted failure. He had a quick word with Craig Oliver, the Downing Street director of communication. 'You should go', the spin doctor told the prime minister. Cameron heeded the advice (I owe this information to Lord Cooper, interview with the author 8 July 2016).

The beginning of the battle

It had seemed very different just a few months before. To be sure, some academics and pollsters had suggested that 'we would expect the current government to lose the referendum by 4 per cent', and this had even been reported in the *Daily Express* (Qvortrup 2016: 61). But what did experts know about practical politics? Besides, the *Express* was arguably prone to exaggeration. It was the clear conviction among the chattering classes – and among those with money and influence – that Remain would prevail. In early February 2016, Lord Rose, the chair of Britain Stronger in Europe, boldly declared that those favouring continued membership would win by a 'substantial margin' (Jon Stone, *The Independent*, 5 February 2016).

The markets reacted with controlled concern when David Cameron announced the date of the referendum at a press conference on 22 February. The pound fell by 2 per cent – most of all because Boris Johnson (the mayor of London), to everybody's surprise, declared that he would be advocating a vote for 'Brexit'. The man often dubbed the 'clown prince' of the Conservative Party looked almost like a serious politician; he had cut his blond locks and tried to sound statesmanlike as he announced his decision. Cameron seemed unperturbed. And why shouldn't he be? A poll in the *Daily Telegraph* showed 54 per cent for Remain and a mere 46 per cent for Leave (18 February 2016).

The campaign was carefully planned and clinically executed in the first 24 hours. Only a day after Cameron's announcement, a third of the FTSE 100 companies' CEOs signed a letter in *The Times* warning against Brexit. The markets, though, were beginning to show concern. The pound dropped further. The signs of trouble did not seem to affect David Cameron and his team. An opinion poll conducted by YouGov showing 37 per cent for Leave and 36 for Remain – and a massive 27 per cent undecided – did not cause alarm in the high command.

The referendum was not yet the all-consuming issue it later became. And David Cameron was able to bury bad news and control the media. It did not seem coincidental that the figures showing increased immigration came out on 25 February, the day when the BBC had to admit that the sexual abuse committed by the disgraced DJ Jimmy Savile had been more widespread than hitherto reported. But immigration was Cameron's Achilles' heel, and *The Guardian*'s interview with Iain Duncan Smith, under the headline 'Cameron's Deal will do nothing to reduce migration', was not welcome. But the issue seemed to be under control.

The opinion polls told a different story, however. Both *The Independent* and *The Economist* published opinion polls showing a lead for Leave. By the beginning of March, the two sides were tied. The small lead for Remain at the beginning of the campaign had evaporated. Philip Hammond, the foreign secretary, was dispatched to counter Leave's claim that Britain could remain a member of the single market. The economic arguments were clearly the Remain side's favoured argument. But, as was becoming increasingly clear, Leave had a simple response to these claims: 'Project Fear'. All predictions were treated with a single but effective response. The 'elites' were scaremongering.

Rather than addressing the concerns – and rather than responding to the challenge – the Brexiteers sensibly chose to respond by counter-claims that the economy would prosper in the event of a vote to leave. The headline in the Brexit-supporting *Daily Telegraph* on 3 March announcing – on the basis of an ill-advised remark by Lord Rose – that 'Wages to rise if we quit the EU' was indicative of the response to the prophecies of gloom peddled by the Remain campaign.

By late March, the opinion polls seemed to swing back towards Remain. Maybe the 'scaremongering' – if thus it was – was working? With the benefit of hindsight, one might look for signs that Remain was losing ground. But such signs were difficult to see at the time. Project Fear, if this epithet is appropriate, was working. In a poll conducted by ComRes for Reuter, 55 per cent of the respondents reported that they were worried about the impact of Brexit on the pound.

Seen in the light of other referendums on European integration or EU membership, the Leave campaign was making a number of elementary mistakes at this stage. Michael Gove – the justice secretary – did not help his cause when he made sweeping assertions about the links between the EU and political extremism. The *Sunday Times* headline on 6 March, '"EU fuels terror and Fascism", says Gove', rather smacked of a similar claim by the Dutch government in the ill-fated EU Constitutional referendum in 2005. Back then the voters had punished the government in the Netherlands for making far-fetched claims. At this stage, so it seemed, Gove was committing the same mistake. The polls showed a small – but statistically significant – lead for Remain.

Maybe it was this lead that led to increasingly desperate measures. *The Sun* – a newspaper that made no secret of its visceral dislike of the EU – even tried to cite what it claimed to be the Queen's support for Brexit. The source was reportedly Michael Gove (*The Guardian*, 12 March 2016). The Palace immediately denied the claim. The report in the Murdoch paper was later criticised by the Independent Press Standards Organisation. Whether the (apparently) false views of the Queen convinced any voters is difficult to say. At this stage of the campaign, with three months to go, the Brexiteers were in apparent disarray. On 9 March, the same day as the *Sun* published its controversial headline about the monarch's alleged support for Brexit, Boris Johnson tried to distance himself from an email which – allegedly – was aimed at gagging staff by telling them not to contradict the Mayor of London's views on the benefits of leaving the EU. The Leave campaign was reduced to firefighting and to issuing rather incoherent claims. Meanwhile David Cameron – now getting into his stride as a campaigner – continued to hammer home the message that 'pressure on the pound [would hit] hard working families [who would be] losing their livelihood' if Britain were to leave the EU.

It was looking relatively good for Cameron and his allies. The Remain campaign led by the very able Will Straw – the son of the former Labour foreign and home secretary Jack Straw – was running a confident and professional campaign: there was no need to worry, he told this author in a slick office in the City of London. But there was something not quite right about his cocksure insistence. The power-dressing young professionals in trendy Jack Wills shirts in the Remain office brought back memories of New Labour in the late 1990s: a whiff of arrogance that should have alerted seasoned campaigners that all was not well. Yet the polls did not give the Remain camp cause for concern. Perhaps things were going a bit too well; perhaps it was the whiff of complacency in the air-conditioned office that spelled doom. *The Economist* suggested as much when it noted, 'the campaign to leave the European Union is still behind but is picking up speed'. In a sentence that seemed almost prophetic the paper speculated, 'Mr Cameron must sometimes regret the promise of a referendum he made three years ago' (11 March 2016: 28). This seemed like an over-reaction at the time. The opinion polls suggested a continuing trend towards Remain – though the margin rarely exceeded 4 per cent.

The erosion of the Remain campaign

It is hard to pinpoint the critical event and changes with anything like mathematical accuracy. Referendums are rarely decided by cataclysmic events but rather by gradual erosion. When George Osborne, the chancellor of the exchequer, duly presented his budget on 16 March, it seemed like a political set piece. The formally neutral and independent Office of Budget Responsibility duly warned of the negative effects of Brexit (Office of Budget Responsibility 2016). Predictably, the markets responded well to the budget. But it is one thing to present a sound and credible macroeconomic picture, it is quite another to reassure voters – especially those with the most to lose. The budget – though the media was slow to pick up on this – contained cuts to disability benefits as well as tax cuts for the wealthier. This prompted Iain Duncan Smith – the secretary of state for work and pensions – to resign. In his resignation letter, the prominent Brexiteer made clear that the cuts were 'not defensible in the way they were placed within a Budget that benefits higher earning taxpayers'

('Iain Duncan Smith resignation letter', in BBC, *Today* programme, 18 March 2016).

While Iain Duncan Smith conceded that 'difficult cuts have been necessary', another budget skewed against the interests of poorer and older citizens gave Osborne and Cameron a credibility problem. This problem was made worse three weeks later when it was revealed that David Cameron's father was named in the Panama Papers. This was a leak of 11.5 million files from the database of the world's fourth biggest offshore law firm, Mossack Fonseca in Panama. It revealed how the superrich — including family members of leading politicians — were hiding money in various tax-havens. While the prime minister had not committed any offence, the impression that he had benefited from his father's fund effectively thwarted any claims that Cameron and Osborne could credibly speak for the common voter.

A political leader, observed Aristotle, needs to have moral authority to persuade his audience, and he gets this when his speech is delivered in such as manner as to render him worthy of confidence' (Aristotle 2006: 17). The resignation of Iain Duncan Smith and the subsequent revelations in the Panama Papers brought back memories of David Cameron and George Osborne as — in the words of Nadine Dorries (a prominent backbencher with working-class roots) — 'two posh boys who don't know the price of milk ... two arrogant posh boys who show no remorse, no contrition, and no passion to want to understand the lives of others' (in BBC, *Today* programme, 23 April 2012). Cameron's image as an Old Etonian was turning into a distinct liability. It was tempting to quote George Orwell (also an alumnus of the said school): 'probably the battle of Waterloo *was* won on the playing-fields of Eton, but the opening battle of all subsequent wars have been lost there. One of the dominant facts of English [and British] life ... has been the decay of ability in the ruling class' (Orwell 2014: 150). For a campaign which aimed at convincing the least well-off that they would be better off financially within the EU, the tax cuts for the rich and the prime minister's and the chancellor's association with very wealthy individuals did damage to their credibility.

Referendums in the United Kingdom are tightly regulated to ensure fairness. Under the Political Parties, Elections and Referendum Act 2000, the Electoral Commission designates two campaigns – one from each side – to conduct the referendum. Under the Act, each side is limited to spend a maximum of £7 million within the official referendum period.

One of the most important moments in the campaign came on 13 April. On this day, the Electoral Commission gave the so-called 'designation' to Britain Stronger in Europe. That was not unexpected. There were no other contenders. But on the other side of the argument there had been a fierce jockeying for position between Leave.eu (supported by Nigel Farage and bankrolled by the businessman Arron Banks) and Vote Leave (with, among others, the Conservatives' Boris Johnson and Michael Gove – and UKIP's only MP Douglas Carswell). The latter got the designation.

As a third party, Leave.eu was limited to spending a maximum of £700,000. However, as UKIP – which was top-down controlled by Farage and Banks – received more than 10 per cent of the votes in the 2015 Westminster election, the party could spend an additional £4 million. The failure to clinch the designation did not prevent UKIP, or Farage, from mounting an efficient campaign. But the split between the two campaigns and the accompanying infighting, animosity and clash of egos were a hindrance for the Brexiteers.

Under the legislation, the campaign period was to last between 15 April and 23 June (the day of the referendum). The government decided to follow the letter rather than the spirit of the legislation. A week before the campaign proper started, HM Treasury distributed a document, which set out what they claimed to be the economic consequences of Brexit. There was outrage over the spending of over £9 million of taxpayers' money on a leaflet that presented a one-sided assessment of the macro-economic impact of non-EU membership. The timing was unfortunate in several ways. The day before, the Dutch voters had rejected the EU's trade deal with the Ukraine in a non-binding referendum, but, worse still, in the following days, there were more revelations about David Cameron's father's private finances, his secret account in Panama – and, by implication, how David Cameron might have benefited from the arrangement. With hindsight, it was admitted, 'the treasury document was a mistake'. Somewhat surprisingly for a professional campaign such as the one the Remain side was running, the document's claims and the wisdom of releasing the report had 'not been tested in focus groups' (Lord Cooper, interview with the author, 8 July 2016). Before the campaign, it was the received wisdom that economic uncertainty favoured the Remain campaign. But conveying this message to the voters was a difficult task. After the campaign, it was admitted that the document had backfired (Lord Cooper, interview with the author, 18 July 2016).

The economic argument – and why it failed

Practically all respected economists and financial institutions (from Goldman Sachs through the International Monetary Fund and the Bank of England to the Institute of Fiscal Studies) warned against the consequences of Brexit, and no prominent economist of the Nobel Prize calibre supported the Brexit supporters' rosy optimism. This presented a problem for the Leave campaign. Without any economist of note on its side it faced an uphill struggle. It resolved this by resorting to the claim that the UK taxpayers transferred £350 million a week to the EU. The claim was dismissed by the government and HM Treasury – as one would expect. The assertion was also dismissed by the UK Statistics Authority, whose chair, Sir Andrew Dilnot, in unequivocal terms denounced the claim: 'UK Statistics Authority is disappointed to note that there continue to be suggestions that the UK contributes £350 million to the EU each week, and that this full amount could be spent elsewhere.' The Treasury Committee in the House of Commons also denounced the claim that Britain was transferring this amount of money to the EU, noting that the 'real' figure was closer to £180 million a week.

Unperturbed, and in spite of being challenged, Vote Leave

repeated the £350 million assertion and even printed it on the side of its battle-bus. It also made the claim that this amount could be better spent on the NHS. 'When you tell a great lie and repeat it often, then people will believe it in the end', an infamous spin-doctor once noted (Goebbels 1934). This seems to have been true for the £350 million claim. The Remain side was in a bind. And it was powerless to do anything; 'the other side had the best line and the best lies', as one prominent Remain campaigner put it. 'People [in focus groups] would spontaneously quote the £350 million a week. We would then tell them that this was not true, but when they were told about the real figure they would still say, "yes, but that is also a lot"' (Lord Cooper, interview with the author, 18 July 2016).

Referendum campaigns are never fought in a vacuum. Alongside the fierce debate, there were other stories in the media. Leicester FC (the 5000–1 outsiders) won the football Premier League, and more importantly from a political point of view there were elections in London, Scotland and Wales. These campaigns had not been quiet affairs. David Cameron faced the problem of having to fight the referendum as a unifying figure, and, at the same time, to contest candidate elections in the devolved regions. The prime minister's campaign against Labour's candidate Sadiq Khan – the son of a Pakistan-born bus driver – and his subtle assertion that the Muslim politician was linked to extremists backfired. Labour won the mayoral election in London but the party suffered a humiliating loss when it was beaten into third place in Scotland.

The battle in the elections to the devolved parliaments was a distraction. Further it sowed divisions and resulted in animosities between individuals and parties who needed to establish trust and build bridges. With six weeks to go, Labour, Conservative and Scottish National politicians were struggling to work effectively together. One of the main problems for the campaign was the near-absence of the Labour leader Jeremy Corbyn. The leftist firebrand had never been a great admirer of the EU in the first place. Asked how much he supported the EU on a scale from 0 to 10, he told the comedy programme *The Last*

Leg, 'well, about seven and a half'. That the Labour leader's most substantial comment was uttered on a satirical programme was indicative of his involvement.

Labour was in disarray, and Jeremy Corbyn – and his staff – refused to be on message. The Labour leader who – reportedly – had no communication with the Remain campaign dismissed carefully crafted statements intended to address Labour voters' concerns (Lord Cooper, interview with the author, 18 July 2016). These problems did not translate into the polls. From late April to the middle of May, the Remain side enjoyed a sustained and increased lead in the polls. It was as if the economic arguments were finally working. International leaders warned against Brexit. Five former general secretaries of NATO warned against Britain leaving the EU and so did eleven former US Security chiefs including George Shultz (Republican) and Madeleine Albright (Democrat). The campaign was going well for those campaigning to stay in the EU.

'Referendums are not kissing babies or shaking hands', said Gerry Gunster (Gerry Gunster, interview with the author, 6 July 2016). The American political consultant had a point. Candidate elections are about trust; about choosing a representative who can speak on behalf of the voters. In parliamentary and presidential elections, we are – with certain exceptions – reluctant to choose individuals whose moral judgements differ from recognised values. The same is not true for direct democracy and votes on policy issues. A referendum does not commit adultery, does not take bribes and it does not file dodgy tax returns. A referendum is about an issue; the Remain campaign failed to realise this and attacked Boris Johnson. To focus on attacking the charismatic Tory politician was a mistake. It only served to move the debate away from the main focus of the campaign.

While the members of the government – and of the political and media elite – were busy attacking Johnson, for 'his fundamentally dishonest gymnastics' (in the words of Sir Nicholas Soames, Winston Churchill's grandson), the Leave campaign became more policy-oriented (*The Independent*, 15 May 2016).

They began to use the immigration card. Earlier in May, Sir John Major had been dispatched to attack the more or less overtly xenophobic tone among some Leave campaigners. In an interview with the *Guardian*, the former Conservative prime minister had told the newspaper that 'as the "leave" arguments implode one by one, some of the Brexit leaders morph into UKIP and turn to their default position; immigration' (quoted in *The Guardian*, 12 May 2016).

Whether this was, indeed, a sign of desperation, as suggested by the former prime minister, was debatable. The £350 million claim was still convincing to many 'ordinary voters'. And immigration was a potent weapon, though not necessarily a pleasant one. Sir John's intervention seemed to have backfired. Immigration had been relatively absent from the debate until then. Boris Johnson had raised the issue in late April, but with little effect. Major's having accused the Leave side of xenophobia did not tarnish the Brexiteers. Rather it made immigration a salient issue.

Further, the immigration issue showed David Cameron's impotence vis-à-vis other European leaders. When Iain Duncan Smith told *The Sun* that the German chancellor Angela Merkel had vetoed a British proposal for an 'immigration lock', it did not only raise the immigration issue even further, it also showed that David Cameron was a weak leader who had failed to negotiate anything approaching a deal that could satisfy a British electorate who felt that immigration levels had risen way above what they regarded as the acceptable level.

Referendums are about framing the debate. Commercials and advertising may not be able to tell people what to think. But an effective campaign can be successful in telling people what to think about. At the risk of sounding theoretical, it is instructive to quote the political scientist Ece Atikcan's conclusion from her survey of several EU referendums. 'Politicians', she observed, 'attempt to mobilize voters behind their policies by encouraging them to think along particular lines, emphasizing certain features of these policies. These frames organize everyday reality by providing meaning to events and [by] promoting particular definitions and interpretations of political issues. The influences these frames have on the voter is the framing effect' (Atikcan 2015: 18).

The Leave campaigns were a textbook example of this. Gerry Gunster was in no doubt that the 'framing' of the debate effectively won the campaign. 'It was to be a people's campaign', he says. And, unlike the Remain campaign, both the official and the unofficial Leave campaigns had a simple message. 'We can't remember the slogan for remain. That says it all. But months after this campaign people will remember "I want my country back"' (Gerry Gunster, interview with the author, 6 July 2016). Similarly Vote Leave, the officially designated campaign, used the slogan, 'Take back control'. This simple slogan – coupled with the aforementioned claim that Britain paid £350 million a week to the EU – gave the Leave campaign an edge.

In his prescient book *The Revolt of the Elites*, the American commentator Christopher Lasch lamented how 'the elites who define the issues have lost touch with the people' (Lasch 1996: 3). The referendum campaign was characterised by this chasm between the experts and the urban cosmopolitan elite and those whom Nigel Farage called 'good people, honest people, decent people'.

The official Remain campaign fundamentally failed to understand how the voters' attitudes were shaped by an active dislike of experts and various elite representatives who told people what to think. Voters were not impressed when – on 20 May – the singer Paloma Faith, the actor Benedict Cumberbatch and the author John le Carré urged voters to vote Remain. Nor were the voters – or a majority of them – convinced by the scientist Stephen Hawking's suggestion that a vote for Leave would hurt British science and research, let alone by the former footballer David Beckham's recommendation to 'vote remain'.

Seemingly oblivious to the celebrities' failure to convince the voters in other referendums, the Remain campaign dispatched the comedian Eddie Izzard to tour the country with a 'positive' message and to tell voters about the economic benefits of EU membership. This barrage of arguments for Remain from celebrities contained warnings about the economy – warnings that were constantly repeated by economists and international institutions. But the technical arguments did not help Remain. Wavering voters were not responding to the predictions of economic gloom presented by David Cameron and his allies.

By the end of May immigration emerged as the big issue in the campaign. Many in the 'elites' believed this hurt the Leave campaign. It did not. In the first weekend of May, Nigel Farage emerged after two weeks' self-imposed silence. He did so with a claim that the sexual attacks in Cologne on New Year's Eve would not have happened without the existence of the borderless Schengen area. (Schengen is the name for the area within the EU where citizens can travel across borders without showing their passport.) Strictly speaking, this meant that similar attacks were unthinkable as Britain is not part of this area. But such subtleties were lost on his supporters. And, worse still for his opponents, they took his bait. Two days later Justin Welby, the archbishop of Canterbury, criticised 'Farage without hesitation'. This suited the UKIP leader. On the same day, 7 June, sensing that the economic argument had been exhausted, Farage told *ITV News*, 'there is more to life than GDP'. The argument seemed to chime with the feeling in the country, especially among the older generation.

Opinion polls and focus group research had long shown a generational gap between pro-EU younger voters and Eurosceptic older citizens. This provided another headache for Remain. It was assumed that most of the unregistered voters were young – or first-time voters. When the voter registration site crashed on the day of the deadline, Parliament voted through emergency legislation to extend the deadline by 48 hours. *The Daily Mail* described the decision to enfranchise voters as 'undemocratic': a decision that could have been presented as extending democracy to younger voters was perceived as the 'elite's' attempt to move the goalposts. The Leave side was powering ahead. With two weeks to go before the referendum the Brexiteers were marginally ahead.

With ten days to go, Remain relaunched its campaign with a speech by Gordon Brown. The former prime minister, who was credited with saving the Union after his late intervention in the

2014 Scottish referendum, was to give a speech. 'A campaign that's winning never needs a relaunch', was the laconic and stinging comment by Tory Brexiteer Dr Liam Fox MP. Gordon Brown's speech – and the intervention by the Trades Union Congress the following day – could be dubbed 'too little too late'. The Leave campaign edged further forward and reached a six-point lead. The economic arguments were falling on deaf ears. To add to the Remain campaign's woes, carefully choreographed interventions – such as a joint appearance by George Osborne and his predecessor Alistair Darling – backfired when Jeremy Corbyn contradicted the calibrated message. Meanwhile the immigration issue was getting traction. Nigel Farage unveiled a poster showing Middle Eastern refugees and the caption 'Breaking Point: We must break free of the EU and take back control'. Of course, the Middle Eastern refugees were nothing to do with the EU and could – arguably – be said to be the result of a misguided foreign policy of Britain and America.

The referendum murder

And then it all changed. On 16 June, the thitherto little-known Labour MP Jo Cox was brutally murdered, apparently by a deranged man shouting 'Britain first'. The stock market reacted positively, on the cynical assumption that the killing would give the flagging Remain campaign sympathy. If the traders had cared to read the history of EU referendums they might have thought differently. In 2003, the Swedish foreign minister Anna Lindt had been killed three days before the referendum on the introduction of the euro. Notwithstanding public sympathy, the Swedish voters rejected the adoption of the single currency.

There was a sense that this was different. The Leave campaign was clearly shaken. The murder briefly stalled the momentum towards Leave. The media – with the *Daily Mail* leading the charge – described Jo Cox's killer as 'a loner with a history of mental illness'. When the man appeared in court he gave his name as 'death to traitors – freedom for Britain' rather than his real name Thomas Mair. Many in the liberal media accused Leave in general and Nigel Farage in particular of 'surfing the moral sewer' (Schama 2016: 13).

The market's initial reaction to the murder of Jo Cox seemed warranted as the campaign began again after three days of mourning. The Remain camp was in front – albeit by a mere three points. And *The Sun* – sensing that the murder had changed the game – editorialised that there 'has been a conscious decision and deplorable move by some in the Remain camp to turn the vote into a moral crusade [and] exploit a nation still mourning a much loved MP' (20 June 2016). If this was sour grapes, they were premature. In the few remaining days of the campaign, the murder was, if not forgotten, then at least relegated to a subordinate role; behind the economy, the 'take back control' mantra and immigration.

The result

On 23 June, 46 million voters were eligible to vote – and £45 million had been placed in bets. The polls closed at 10 pm. Ten hours later David Cameron had resigned – and no hours and three minutes later Nigel Farage admitted that the £350 million claim was 'a mistake' (*Daily Telegraph*, 24 June 2016). But at this stage he and the Leave side(s) had already won the campaign. The turnout in the referendum was just over 72 per cent: 51.9 per cent voted to leave the EU.

What had happened? Who had voted Remain and who had supported the Leave side? The pollsters had a clear picture. Immigration had been the main motivating factor. So why did Cameron and Remain not counter the claims? Because, says Lord Cooper, there was little they could do: 'Ten days out and we considered a vow but we decided against it. We couldn't say anything that was remotely close to what they [the voters] wanted' (Lord Cooper, interview by the author, 18 July 2016).

Treating the voters as a monolithic block is, needless to say, sociologically illegitimate. No two voters are the same

Table 3   Demographic drivers of Leave/Remain vote shares
(Pearson's correlation coefficients)

Leave vote share v. UKIP vote in 2015	R = 0.81
Leave vote v. English only (or Welsh only)	R = 0.51
Leave vote v. 'not in very good health'	R = 0.55
Leave vote share v. non-professional occupation	R = 0.74
Leave vote share v. socio-economic group	R = −0.65

All significant at p >0.01, N: 1200, Data courtesy of Populus

but certain patterns appear when the mass of the citizens is compared. There were no end of fanciful correlations and calculations undertaken by the pollsters. Populus – who also did the polling for David Cameron – said in an internal memo that support for Leave was correlated with obesity. In crass terms – and without qualifying caveats – Britain would still have been a member of the European Union if the Britons weren't so fat! Of course, this conclusion is somewhat frivolous. Obesity is a social phenomenon which is highly correlated with poverty measures. Statisticians use a measure known as the Pearson's Correlation Coefficient. A perfect mathematical correlation is $R = 1.0$ and no correlation is $R = 0$. Conventionally any figure above $R = 0.3$) is considered strong. (The following figures are courtesy of Populus, statistically significant at 0.01.) The same pollsters found a correlation between non-professional occupation and Leave of $R = 0.74$ and a negative correlation of Leave vote share and socio-economic group of $R = − 0.65$: in other words, the higher the social group the lower the propensity to vote Leave. When the Leave vote share was correlated with years of education, the figures show a correlation of $R = 0.80$. On these measures, education was a better predictor of the voter's attitude towards the EU than was support for UKIP in the last general election.

But for all the correlations and statistical calculations, pollsters failed to predict the result. As in the general election in 2015, there was an initial discrepancy between online and telephone polls. In the early stages of the referendum, the same tendency was apparent. YouGov – which does online polling only – had a consistently larger lead for Leave than IPSOS/Mori and other companies that mainly or exclusively conduct their polls face-to-face or over the telephone. But over the campaign this discrepancy disappeared. At the end of the campaign no one was much the wiser and most of the projections – apart from econometrics-based calculations as undertaken by this author (Qvortrup 2016) – were imprecise estimates.

Is God a Brexiteer? Is the Norse thunder-god Thor? One thing was certain: if a deity is responsible for the weather, she or he seemed predisposed for the Leave side. An almighty thunderstorm caused flooding, and the *Financial Times* speculated that the bad weather would benefit the fired-up UKIP supporters. The view was shared – with hindsight – by the Remain camp. 'The weather in London lost us votes', according to Andrew Cooper (interview with the author, 8 July 2016). Nevertheless, camp Cameron expected to win. As we know now, they did not. Nigel Farage – rejuvenated after he had completed his lifetime ambition – was triumphant when he faced the media on the morning of Friday 24 June. A politician who had never been a member of the House of Commons, the former stockbroker, whose entire political career was built in Strasbourg and Brussels, had succeeded in getting Britain out of the EU. His erstwhile colleagues in the City and at other financial centres around the world were less impressed. The pound was in free fall and dropped from 1.48 against the US dollar to 1.36 – and continued to fall after that. The stock market nosedived. In the first twelve hours after the result the stock market lost more than Britain's annual contribution to the EU budget. Even the *Daily Express* – normally a bastion of self-confident national(ist) pride – conceded that 'France "overtakes UK as world's fifth largest economy" after pound plunges' (24 June 2016). Following a weekend of turmoil, Standard and Poor, followed by Moody (credit rating agencies whose ratings determine the price at which governments can borrow money on the financial markets), downgraded Britain's credit rating from Triple A to AA. Investment was down by 7 per cent. Many economists felt vindicated. Mervyn King, the former governor of the Bank of England, however, was relaxed: 'Markets go up, markets go down' (*The Andrew Marr Show*, BBC1, 26 June 2016).

David Cameron's gamble had failed. The proverb has long had it that politics always ends in defeat. In Cameron's case it was self-inflicted. Of course, not all blame can be laid at his door, though it was he who called the referendum. But ultimately, it was the majority of the voters who took the decision to leave the EU. It is tempting to cite John Dryden's (1631–1700) lines from 'Absalom and Achitophel':

> Nor is the People's Judgement always true
> The most may err as grossly as the few.
>
> (Dryden 1681: Pt I, lines 781–2)

But, of course, others may conclude that the people did not 'err' and that 'Brexit' was an opportunity of a lifetime: a chance to shake off the shackles of regulation, to 'take back control'.

Was the British referendum a typical example of a referendum? Was this conclusive proof that government by referendum is bound to be a bad idea for a government in power? This is a question we shall return to in the last chapter.

The myth of populist referendums

IN 1992, Frederik W. de Klerk, the president of South Africa, was in trouble. Nelson Mandela had been released from prison and there were signs that South Africa would finally end the apartheid regime, which had made the country an international pariah. Not all whites were happy with de Klerk. His National Party was losing by-elections and this threatened the legitimacy of the process towards ending apartheid. The president reacted resolutely. He needed a mandate and he needed to regain momentum. He called a referendum, in which the white South Africans were asked the question, 'Do you support continuation of the reform process which the State President began on February 2, 1990 and which is aimed at a new constitution through negotiations' (quoted in Loizides 2016: 127). The gamble worked: 68 per cent of the voters endorsed the president – albeit after a campaign in which major companies threatened to leave the country in the event of a 'no' vote. Indeed, General Tire threatened the retrenchment of all employees ... as a likely outcome of an unfavourable referendum result (Loizides 2016: 137). But 'Project Fear' – as a similar tactic was later christened – worked (see Chapter 3). As de Klerk noted in his autobiography, '[the] calculated gamble paid off handsomely' (de Klerk 1999: 234). Sometimes resoluteness – what political theorists like Machiavelli and Hannah Arendt call *Virtù* (Arendt 1968: 153) – is rewarded; sometimes the world favours the bold. And, sometimes it does not. Twenty-four years later the British prime minister David Cameron had, as we saw in the previous chapter, the same idea. Yet unlike de Klerk in South Africa David Cameron counted wrong: 51.9 per cent of the British voters – on a 72 per cent turnout – opted for Leave in the referendum in June 2016 (see previous chapter). What seemed an eminently suitable idea had backfired spectacularly. The referendum on British membership of the EU ended in agony – for the prime minister, at least.

Of course not all politicians submitting issues to the voters suffer the same fate. The Russian President Vladimir Putin did not have any worries when – in March 2014 – he submitted the annexation of Crimea to a popular vote and won the approval of 96 per cent of the voters in the territory. He was not the only authoritarian leader to seek the endorsement of the voters. Two months before, the Egyptian leader Abdel Fattah el-Sisi had shown the way when he duly received 98 per cent support for a new constitution (Qvortrup 2014).

As these examples suggest, 'the use of referendums around the world has proliferated remarkably in the past 30 years' (Tierney 2012: 4). Why are more and more issues submitted to the voters? How does this square with the overall health of democracy? Is the growing use of referendums an indication of authoritarian leaders' penchant for bypassing legislatures? And is the decision to go straight to 'the people' an indication of growing populism?

Certainly, votes in recent years in what the American organisation Freedom House categorise as Partly Free countries like Bolivia under Evo Morales, in Ecuador under Rafael Correa and in Sassou Nguesso's Congo-Brazzaville suggest that semi-authoritarian rulers have an inclination to seek a direct mandate from the people. Add to this the referendum initiated by Viktor Orbán on the EU's immigration policy in Hungary in the autumn of 2016, and it is easy to conclude that referendums have gone from being a shield against executive dominance to being a weapon in the hands of the executive. To draw such a conclusion from a handful of conspicuous cases would, however, be hasty and unwarranted. Whether referendums and plebiscites have become more associated with populism and semi-authoritarian tendencies requires an analysis of all the votes held in different countries since 1973.

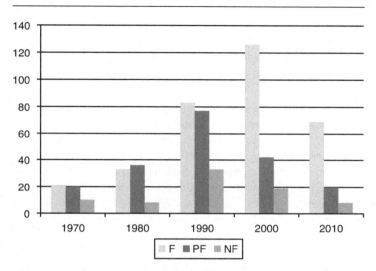

Figure 1   Total number of referendums and plebiscites in Free, Partly Free and Not Free states 1973–2016

This analysis runs the risk of not comparing like with like. There is something odd about comparing votes held in what Freedom House describes as Free societies with ones held in Partly Free and even Not Free countries. That these votes are described by the same term suggests that the word 'referendum' is so broad that it borders on being analytically meaningless. To make sense of the these votes it is useful to follow the distinction often made in the French literature, according to which the 'referendum allows the people to express themselves freely, [whereas] the plebiscite allows a person ... to legitimize him or herself by posing a question to the people who answer in the affirmative' (Guillaume-Hofnung 1987: 14).

Using Freedom House data, we can categorise the different types of votes depending on the type of regime in question. Figure 1 shows the distribution of nationwide votes in Free, Partly Free and Not Free states in the period 1973–2016. Since 1973 there have been a total of 605 votes, out of which 332 have been referendums, held in countries categorised as Free. (This excludes Switzerland which accounts for half of all nationwide referendums.) The rate of holding referendums in Free states has increased steadily since the early 1970s and reached its zenith in the first decade of the twenty-first century. The number of referendums rose by 51 per cent in Free states between the 1990s and the 2000s and there are indications that a similar level will be reached in the second decade of this century. So far there has been an average of 11.5 nationwide referendums in Free states per year in the second decade of the new millennium, only slightly below the average of 12.6 per year in the decade before.

Leaders in competitive autocracies have often been associated with a growing use of plebiscites – just think the myriad of votes in Kyrgyzstan (seven were held under Askar Akayev) and Bashar al-Assad's taste for submitting policy issues to the people even in the midst of the Syrian civil war (Levitsky and Way 2010). But these selected examples – and the ones mentioned above – are not generally representative of the general trend. Rather, the number of votes held in Partly Free states has dropped considerably since the high point in the 1990s. Thus there was a 45 per cent decrease in the number of votes held in Partly Free states between the 1990s and the 2000s. In the same period there was also a 42 per cent decrease in the number of plebiscites in Not Free states. Statistically speaking, there is a stark contrast between the tendencies in Free states and the states that fall below this threshold. Referendums have grown in number in the former but have become less common in Partly Free and Not Free states. These two different trends require different explanations.

Referendums in democracies

What accounts for the increase in the number of referendums in Free states like the United Kingdom? The causes may be manifold, and undoubtedly each referendum follows a unique trajectory based on exceptional circumstances. David Cameron's decision to allow a vote on Scottish independence in 2014 was

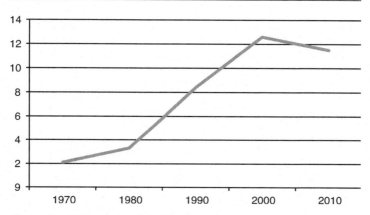

Figure 2   Average number of referendums per year in Free states 1973–2016

very different from Italian prime minister Matteo Renzi's decision to hold a vote on a new constitution in 2016.

It is noteworthy that the number of referendums in Free states has grown consistently since the 1970s, and even before that time. As Figure 2 shows, there has been a steady growth in the number of referendums since the beginning of the 1970s, which is in contrast to the modest use of referendums from the 1920s until the 1960s (see Figure 3).

Without there being a perfect correlation or direct association, it is striking that the increase followed in the wake of changes in the party systems in Free states, namely tendencies towards post-materialist voting and partisan dealignment. (Post-materialist values are the issues that came on the agenda in the 1970s. Previously, most political issues were 'materialist' – had to do with economic matters. Now, with higher levels of material well-being, voters were free to turn their attention to post-materialist values such as women's rights and environmental issues. 'Partisan dealignment' was a political scientists' term for the decline of political tribalism. Previously, most voters were 'party-identifiers' and followed 'their' party almost no matter what. Now, they became 'dealigned', and began to change

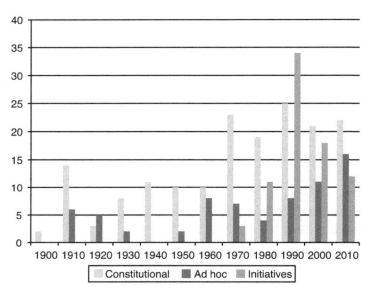

Figure 3   Referendums in democratic countries: constitutional, ad hoc and citizens' initiatives 1900–2016

parties.) Since the early 1970s more voters have been inclined to shift parties, and political scientists have talked about an increase in electoral volatility (Dassonneville 2012). Before 'dealignment' political parties were relatively free to pursue policies without fear of losing core supporters. But, as new issues came on to the agenda – such as environmental protection and EU membership – governments became more willing to use provisions for referendums for fear of alienating supporters. Political parties, according to this hypothesis, submitted issues to the voters that were 'too hot to handle' (Matsusaka 1992: 542). This resulted in referendums on post-materialist issues like nuclear power (Italy, Sweden, Austria and Bulgaria), gay marriage (Ireland, Croatia and Slovenia) and more than forty referendums on European integration or EU membership between 1972 and 2016.

It could be objected that this hypothesis conveniently ignores the fact that referendums in 'Free' polities are held under different provisions and are initiated by very different actors. The propensity to hold referendums for fear that voters will punish political parties that go against them holds true for ad hoc referendums that are initiated voluntarily by governments. But some referendums are constitutionally mandated, and voters themselves initiate others.

Thus, once again, it is prudent to make a distinction between different analytical categories. Some referendums are held as a result of constitutional constraints and are a shield to protect citizens from legislative haste. For example, the 1951 referendum on banning the Communist Party in Australia was held following a ruling by the High Court of Australia, which held the Communist Party Dissolution Act 1950 to be unconstitutional (Australian Communist Party *v* Commonwealth 83 CLR 1, 9 March 1951) and resulted in a vote against government policy. Referendums like this can be categorised as constitutional referendums. Conversely, the Norwegian referendum on whether to join the EU in 1994 and the Maltese referendum on divorce in 2011 were held because the respective governments felt politically compelled to hold them. Votes on ordinary issues not required by the constitution can be categorised as ad hoc referendums. And, as if to make matters even more complicated, yet another category exists: referendums or citizens' initiatives triggered when citizens have gathered a specified number of signatures to force a public vote on an issue. The latter can be categorised as initiatives or citizen-initiated referendums.

With the advent of political leaders who espouse so-called populist policies one would expect to have seen a rise in the number of ad hoc referendums: votes on controversial issues held to appeal to large sections of society who are perceived to be disenfranchised by the 'established' political class. Such votes have taken place: the referendums on the European bailout initiated by the leftist Syriza government in Greece in 2015 and the Polish referendum on a change of the electoral system in 2015 are but two examples.

There has been an increase in the number of ad hoc referendums since the 1970s. However, it is equally clear that constitutional referendums have consistently outnumbered these statistically and continue to do so. Contrary to the impression perhaps given by the media, recent referendums have not generally been votes by populists to overturn the status quo. Rather most referendums have been, and continue to be, those mandated by the constitution.

This, incidentally, is consistent with the work of A.V. Dicey (1835–1922), the English legal theorist who, as we saw earlier, first developed a normative constitutional theory of referendums. In his view the *raison d'être* of this institution was that it should be a 'people's veto', which would prevent 'the passing of any important Act which does not command the sanction of the electors' (Dicey 1981: cix).

Why have referendums been used as a constitutional safeguard? Why have politicians allowed this? One reason could be a greater tendency towards judicial activism? For example, in Ireland – a country with almost annual referendums – the Supreme Court's intervention in the 1980s has meant that a large number of relatively mundane issues have been submitted to the voters (Crotty *v* An Taoiseach, IESC, 9 April 1987). But constitutional referendums have not been confined to countries with activist courts. They have also been increasingly common in countries without a tradition of judicial intervention such as Denmark and Sweden.

That governments have been more willing to hold constitutional referendums in recent decades might be due to political developments and not just (as in Ireland) due to pressure from the judiciary. Constitutional referendums in Denmark and Sweden were held not as a result of court interventions but rather because the party systems in both of these countries have become exceptionally volatile with the emergence of electorally successful populist parties.

In Denmark three constitutional referendums have been held since 2010. Notwithstanding the Danish High Court's refusal to rule on constitutional matters regarding referendums, successive Danish governments have chosen to hold referendums on female royal succession (2009), on whether to join the International Unified Patent Court (2014) and on European police co-operation

(2015). All the issues were opposed by the new political parties the Liberal Alliance and the Danish People's Party. Failure to hold these referendums would – arguably – have been politically costly. Hence changes in the party-system were indirectly responsible for the growth of constitutional referendums.

Referendums, whether ad hoc or constitutional, have been used to keep the elected politicians in check. But not all referendums are ad hoc or constitutional. What about the seemingly inexorable rise in citizen-initiated referendums? As Figure 3 shows, there has been an exceptional increase in the number of these votes. Can citizen-initiated referendums be explained as a result of changes in the party systems?

Citizen-initiated referendums come in two forms: initiatives (which allow voters to propose legislation) and citizen-initiated referendums (which allow voters to hold a vote on an already enacted law or bills before they are promulgated).

Unlike in the United States – where roughly half of the states have them – provisions for citizen initiatives are rare in Free states; they exist only in Hungary, the Netherlands, New Zealand, Latvia, Lithuania, Slovakia, Uruguay and, of course, Switzerland. Apart from Switzerland virtually no citizen initiative has resulted in legislative changes in Free states. Generally this is because of harsh turnout requirements or, as in the cases of the Netherlands and New Zealand, because these votes are advisory only, though initiatives have passed in Uruguay and Hungary.

The relative rarity of initiatives is also true for citizen-initiated referendums, that is, a provision that allows citizens to veto bills provided they can gather a specified number of signatures. Apart from Switzerland, such provisions exist only in Italy and Slovenia. Notwithstanding their relative rarity, there was an explosive growth in the number of citizen-initiated votes from the 1970s until the 1990s, and a declining tendency after that time. This was largely down to single-country factors, above all in Italy.

In the 1970s, the Italian Parliament ratified the hitherto unimplemented Article 75 of the 1946 constitution. The implementation of the so-called *referendum abrogativo* allows five hundred thousand citizens to demand a referendum on any existing law. The reason for implementing the legislation was tactical: to resolve a disagreement over divorce legislation between the Christian Democrats and smaller parties in the coalition. The parties agreed to disagree by submitting the issue to a referendum. As an unforeseen consequence of the legislation, activists began to employ the provision to challenge existing legislation on state funding of political parties, immunity from prosecution and the electoral system, which underpinned the Italian Second Republic (Uleri 2002). In all, 46 abrogative referendums were held between 1974 and 1999. The dramatic increase in the number of citizen-initiated referendums is not, therefore, part of a generic trend but can in large measure be explained by exceptional circumstances in Italy.

The charge that referendums are prone to result in populist measures might in part be supported by the citizen-initiated votes held in the remaining countries that allow referendums initiated by the voters. The non-binding citizen-initiated referendum in 2016 in the Netherlands, on whether to ratify the EU's trade agreement with Ukraine, is an example of a vote which arguably used populist sentiment to challenge government policy. That citizen-initiated votes can be contrary to liberal opinion is also shown by the No vote in a citizen initiative that would have legalised same-sex marriage in Slovenia.

More often than not the consequences of citizen-initiated referendums have been minimal. Since 1990, all citizens' initiatives in Latvia, Lithuania and Hungary have been declared invalid for failing to meet the 50 per cent turnout threshold. The same was also true for the citizen-initiated referendums in Italy until 2011. However, after 16 years of failed referendums, the so-called *legittimo impedimento* (a law introduced to prevent a trial against then prime minister Berlusconi) was abrogated by 95 per cent of the voters on a 57 per cent turnout. The media-tycoon-turned-politician was forced to resign, later faced a trial and was convicted; a populist politician, who had used citizen-initiated referendums to pave the way to a political career, had fallen victim of a direct democratic institution. Thus most referendums (in a democracy), irrespective of their constitutional form, have been used to limit, constrain and hold in check the power of elected leaders. Plebiscites (in a dictatorship), of course, are a different story.

Plebiscites

Notwithstanding tendencies towards 'the Democratic recession' (Diamond 2015), the frequency of plebiscites has gone down in recent years. As Figure 4 shows, the average number of plebiscites in Partly Free and Not Free states has dropped since the 1990s. The question is: what accounts for the lower propensity to submit issues to votes in authoritarian or semi-authoritarian states? Explaining dictators' or competitive authoritarian leaders' declining tendency to submit issues to plebiscites requires an understanding of why they are – or were – held at all. What, after all, is the point of holding a vote the result of which is in all likelihood a foregone conclusion?

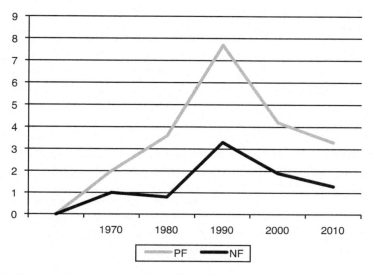

Figure 4   Average annual number of plebiscites in Not Free and Partly Free states 1970–2010

Again, distinctions are important. Plebiscites in Not Free states are held not merely to confer legitimacy upon an autocratic regime but also to signal the total control of the authoritarian government. As Juan Linz observed 'plebiscites [are held to] test the effectiveness of the party and its success in getting out the vote' (Linz 2000: 92). In earlier epochs – before efficient mass surveillance – plebiscites served a useful function of control. This might explain why they were used in totalitarian regimes such as under Adolf Hitler (1933, 1934, 1936 and 1938), Benito Mussolini (1929), Erich Honecker (1971) and Nicolae Ceaușescu (1986) and why former communist *apparatchiks* like Nursultan Nazarbayev in Kazakhstan and Alexander Lukashenko in Belarus were eager to show their continued control through plebiscites.

But plebiscites are no longer in vogue in Not Free states: as Figure 4 shows, their number has dropped, and has done so from a relatively low base. The reasons for this cannot be summarised in a couple of lines, perhaps because plebiscites are a relatively inefficient signifier of total control in the age of cyber-surveillance. (Schneider 2011). As Figures 1 and 4 show, plebiscites in Not Free states always constituted a minority. There were – after 1970 at any rate – always a larger number of votes in Partly Free states than in Not Free states. Of course, each plebiscite has its own aetiology and is driven by distinctive and often unique circumstances. And yet there are certain recurrent patterns.

As a general rule, plebiscites in semi-authoritarian systems do provide a mechanism for gaining legitimacy, albeit under less than ideal circumstances. In the empirical single-country literature, it is often noted that plebiscites held in semi-autocratic regimes, in addition to showing internal support, serve the function of external legitimising. Writing about Ferdinand Marcos's plebiscites in 1975, Noble noted that there were 'were two audiences, one in the Philippines, which continued to include outspoken dissidents, and another in the U.S. Congress, which contained critics threatening to withhold aid from the regime' (Noble 1976: 179). The same explanation is arguably equally convincing for more recent votes in semi-authoritarian regimes.

Most plebiscites in Partly Free states have been held within a few years of an autocrat gaining power, as was the case with Alberto Fujimori in Peru, immediately after his coup in 1993, and Hugo Chávez in Venezuela, in 1999 and 2000. Especially after coming to power it is necessary for competitive autocrats to show that the citizens at large support them. One way of doing this is by holding plebiscites. In 'competitive authoritarian regimes, formal democratic institutions are widely viewed as the principal means of obtaining and exercising political authority' (Levitsky and Way 2002). Plebiscites superficially serve the same function as referendums in Free countries. The difference is that, in Partly Free states, popular votes are held only when this is deemed desirable by the regime. But the longer these rulers are in power the less likely such measures are to win approval. Plebiscites in 'Partly Free' states were lost in Uruguay in 1980 and Chile in 1988 (Altman 2011: 105). As competitive authoritarian systems get more consolidated, they have less need to seek approval. Perhaps, we can but speculate, the risks of holding such votes are too high.

Much as there has been talk about populism and a move away from constitutional government, the use of referendums has not generally been part of this trend. The total number of plebiscites in dictatorships has fallen drastically, and constitutional referendums continue to outnumber ad hoc referendums; votes held by populist leaders have generally fared rather badly. It is empirically speaking a myth that authoritarian or semi-authoritarian rulers have dominated recent referendums and that populists have used this institution to overturn the status quo. While individual examples could be cited, these are exceptions to the rule that the referendum tends to have the effect of a democratic safeguard. Its many shortcomings notwithstanding, the referendum is, on balance, a mechanism for strengthening democracy and has proved to be the people's shield even when governments use it as a sword for gaining more power.

Concluding unscientific postscript

> The referendum is, or may be, an education in the applica-
> tion of men's understandings to the weightiest of political
> concerns – namely the passing of laws – such as is abso-
> lutely unobtainable by voters who are trained to think that
> their role or duty as citizens consists in supporting the
> conservative or radical party, and ... their blind acceptance
> of every proposed enactment which happens to form part
> of the party platform. (Dicey 1890: 508)

THIS is how a Victorian proponent of the referendum summed
up the hopes for this institution. More than a hundred years on,
there are reasons to treat his optimism with scepticism, though it
cannot be entirely dismissed. There is a place for the referendum
but the institution must be used with caution. Dicey, of course,
was not quite as innocent as he would have us (or, perhaps, even
himself) believe. A staunch Free Trade Unionist, he developed
an obsession with Irish Home Rule, which he hated, loathed and
despised. His case for the referendum was opportunist: a barrier
against a policy he disliked. His case for the referendum was very
much the last stand of the angry English nationalist.

There is nothing inherently wrong in being an opportunist.
Politics, after all, is a battle of ideas, a verbal and tactical bare-
knuckle fight, which is won by those who can employ political
institutions most skilfully to their own advantage. To dress up as
a democratic idealist is a tried and tested tactic for zealots with
a completely different agenda.

As we saw in Chapter 1, the history of the use of the referendum from the French Revolution to the present day has shown that cold calculation – some just call it *chutzpah* – has been more important than idealistic thinking among those who have instigated referendums. In the nineteenth century none other than Otto von Bismarck was in favour of referendums (in his case over the future of Schleswig-Holstein) and the Danes (who controlled this largely German-speaking territory) were against. However, once the Iron Chancellor had bulldozed the Lilliputian Danish army at the Battle of Dybbøl in 1864, he saw no need for a referendum. Conversely, the Danes now appealed to the right of the people to decide.

This opportunism might give the referendum a bad reputation. Those who see this institution as 'an abdication of the responsibility of the House [of Commons] and of the Government of the day', to use the words of Tristan Garel-Jones, a former Conservative Minister for Europe (House of Commons Debates, 21 February 1992), might feel vindicated by the story of earlier referendums in the United Kingdom. Though, as we shall see, that might be a premature conclusion.

Britain was a late referendum developer. While there were serious discussions about the introduction of the device in the first two decades of the twentieth century, Britain was left behind when referendums were held in many European countries. Yet one can make too much of this. In truth there were very few referendums between 1920 and the 1960s. Those were often constitutional referendums, which were forced upon the governments of countries – such as the revision of the Danish Constitution in 1953 and the Irish constitutional referendum on changing the electoral system in 1959.

During this era there was little reason to have referendums. The voters were loyal to 'their' political parties and the elites were relatively unified around established ideological positions. This changed in the 1960s and the 1970s. New issues split the political parties. In Scandinavia, the Danish and Norwegian Social Democratic Parties split evenly over membership of the European Community (the forerunner of the EU). In both countries idealistic arguments about the commitment to democracy were used as a fig leaf to justify referendums on the issue; the parties 'agreed to disagree' and gave the mostly sceptical voters the opportunity to remain loyal to 'their' party and yet vote against its – EEC-friendly – leaderships. In many ways, the referendum was a genial solution to an intractable problem.

This was also true in the United Kingdom. From the earliest debates in the late Victorian age until the referendum on Brexit, tactical considerations were the key motivator. The story of the 1975 referendum on membership of the EEC is a case in point. This referendum was held not out of concern for due democratic process but because of tactical considerations within the Labour Party. On the face of it this was not a great advertisement for the referendum as a mechanism.

And yet, an unintended by-product of the 1975 referendum, or more specifically the campaign itself, was to give ordinary citizens a chance to participate in politics without being told what to do by the party hierarchy. Moreover, and perhaps more importantly, the campaign in 1975 challenged the tribalism that had characterised the politics of the United Kingdom. Staunch anti-capitalists from the left joined forces with the likes of Enoch Powell on the right of the political spectrum. And, as significantly, moderate Tories campaigned with moderate Labour politicians. Who can forget the photo of Margaret Thatcher – later transformed into an uncompromising Europhobe – in a knitted jumper with all the European flags?

Cynicism is almost always warranted in politics. And the referendum is no exception. Yet it is important to note that the use of this device – perhaps inadvertently – also gave voters a moral argument for a veto against fundamental changes. By the end of the 1990s – when the referendum had once again re-entered political life – it was this much maligned institution that prevented the United Kingdom from joining the euro. In other countries without debates about or a tradition for holding referendums – such as Germany and Belgium – the decision to join the common currency was taken by the elites without much concern for the voters' opposition. In Britain, membership of the euro was effectively prevented by a referendum that was never held. A commitment by the Labour Party in 1996 to holding a referendum on Scottish and Welsh devolution effectively forced Tony Blair to make the same promise regarding the single currency. He never dared to face the voters on this matter – though he was politically committed to the euro. The referendum, therefore, was like 'the dog that didn't bark', in the Sherlock Holmes story. Again this is not exceptional. In the late 1940s, the Americans insisted that the Japanese constitution provided for a referendum. The Japanese were free to establish an army, but the people had to endorse this first in a referendum. Many Japanese politicians have wanted to change Article 94 of the Constitution, but they have not hitherto dared to ask the largely pacifist Japanese electorate for fear that they might lose. The Japanese have never held a nationwide referendum, but this institution has played a key role in the formation of the country's foreign policy after the war.

Overall, therefore – and despite politicians' inclination to use the referendum tactically – this much-criticised institution can perform a vital function as a check on power – and has done so. Few would have found it acceptable if Scotland had gained independence without a referendum (something that was SNP's official policy until the late 1990s). Even those who profess to 'hate the referendum' – as the columnist Steven Richards claimed in a debate with this author on the BBC *Today* programme (7 February 2007) – would (it is fair to assume) accept that the voters north of the border should have a direct say on the matter. In the case of the Scottish referendum it is also widely agreed that the citizens were informed and interested in the issue, in short that they were able to make reasoned decisions about the issue.

Yet the same was not always the case in the Brexit referendum (as we saw in Chapter 3), and perhaps in the referendum on the alternative vote electoral system (as we saw in Chapter 2). While there was a spirited debate in both cases, there was arguably disinformation on both sides and the vote did not provide incontrovertible proof that all voters were aware of the consequences of voting Remain or Leave, or of the virtues or vices of first-past-the-post versus the alternative vote.

After the Brexit referendum – and to a degree before – it was argued that populists had captured the referendum and that political leaders with a demagogical bent were prone to submit issues to referendums. It followed from this that the referendum was in danger of becoming a populist tool. To say that David Cameron made a catastrophic error – from his own perspective as a pro-European Conservative politician – is trite, and perhaps another good reason to quote George Orwell's line from 'The Lion and the Unicorn': 'What was it that at every decisive moment made every British statesman do the wrong thing with so unerring an instinct?' (Orwell 2014: 150).

But one cannot reject the referendum in general just because one disagrees with the way David Cameron blundered into to calling one. The problem with the referendum in Britain is that it allows the political class (more specifically the prime minister) to use it for narrow political purposes. The referendum ought to be a check: an institution that is analogous to a deliberating second chamber – albeit a more democratic (if occasionally less informed) one.

This danger of using the referendum as a bulwark for change was also present in the Turkish referendum in the spring of 2017 (on the implementation of a new presidential constitution that would strengthen the role of Erdoğan, who had previously served in a mainly ceremonial role) – and many years before in the way the referendum was used by French President Charles de Gaulle in the 1960s. Yet those who use this argument against the referendum, those who claim that it is a populist sword wielded against the largely ignorant masses, forget that those who live by the referendum often die by the referendum: the careers of David Cameron, Alex Salmond – and the great Charles de Gaulle himself – were cut short by this institution. Even General Pinochet in Chile – having grown complacent – lost power when he failed to rig the constitutional referendum in 1988. The Chilean Generalissimo later compared himself to Christ, and claimed that the people of his country were animated by the same hatred that had consumed the mob in Jerusalem in the year AD 33.

The politicians and the 'elites' who are still licking their self-inflicted wounds over the Brexit vote perhaps have a too narrow view of referendums generally if they see Cameron's last referendum as being in any way typical of how the institution is used. It is not. From a comparative perspective, the overall development is that the referendum − as a general rule − has performed a healthy function in democratic countries. As we saw in Chapter 4, while there has been an increase in the number of referendums, most of these have − unlike in Britain − been held because written constitutions require that votes should be held before irreversible changes are made to the political system. In most cases the referendum has not been a tool in the hands of the elite but a people's shield.

In Britain (and France) the referendum has tended to be a device used tactically by powerful and unconstrained rulers. In Ireland, by contrast, the referendum is a barrier against change. For the referendum to perform a useful function in a democratic state under the rule of law, it is recommended that it be used exclusively as a people's veto. As Dicey wrote in the introduction to the eighth edition of *An Introduction to the Study of the Law of the Constitution* in 1915:

> The referendum is sometimes described … as 'the People's veto'. This name is a good one; it reminds us that the main use of the referendum is to prevent the passing of any important Act, which does not command the sanction of the electors. (Dicey 1981: cix)

One may agree or disagree over the wisdom − or otherwise − of Brexit; and it is legitimate to have different opinions about the desirability of Scottish independence. One might also disagree over the nature of the debate, the broadcasters' coverage and the use of social media. Referendums are complex and require people to weigh up consequences and arguments most are unfamiliar with. The referendum is far from being a perfect institution but it is − for better or for worse − here to stay. It is unlikely − though, of course, not inconceivable − that we will go back to the days of pure representative democracy.

Given that we now − on certain issues, at least − have

'government by referendum', it seems much more fruitful to discuss and debate when we should have referendums. Should we have special majority requirements, so that a vote becomes void if the turnout is too low (as is the case in Switzerland)? Or should we require that referendums pass only if all the constituent parts of the United Kingdom vote Yes – as in Canada, where all provinces must endorse constitutional changes?

Some want another referendum on Brexit, others hope there will be another referendum on Scottish independence. Some Irish Nationalists want a referendum on a united Ireland. The referendum could be used in all these cases, and it should be. It would be politically unthinkable that politicians could decide to stay in the EU without asking the people. But these specific questions miss the more general point: who should be allowed to call or initiate referendums? Should it be for the prime minister and the cabinet to call referendums? Or should we have referendums if the Lords and the Commons disagree, as was suggested a century ago by Hobson in *The Crisis of Liberalism*?

Could we introduce a mechanism akin to the Danish constitutional provision that allows a minority of MPs to call a referendum on Bills before they receive Royal Assent? Some say that would lead to chaos, yet in the Danish case it is rarely used, seemingly, because it forces the government to take the views of the opposition into consideration.

Or might we be more radical still and introduce what the Italians call *il referendum abrogativo*, which allows five hundred thousand voters to call a referendum on any law on the statute book (though the vote is void if the turnout is below 50 per cent)? Alternatively is there a case for allowing a specified number of citizens to demand a referendum on laws before they become law as they are able to do in Switzerland?

Some might see these proposals as barmy and out of control. Perhaps, they are. This is for the reader to debate with her or his fellow citizens. One thing is certain: in these other countries the referendum is a check on the government; a mechanism that limits its room for manoeuvring. The countries that have used the referendum have generally been more prosperous and have tended to be economically stable (Frey and Stuzer 2000). Denmark and Switzerland – despite their rather radical provisions for referendums – are rich countries with high levels of public spending and a fully developed welfare state. To be sure, Italy is hardly a haven of governability, yet the country did not become markedly less stable economically when the Radical Party began to use the referendum against the corrupt *partitocra-zia* ('partyocracy') in the 1980s and the 1990s.

Of course it is fair to say that the referendum has had rather drastic effects in Italy. As we saw in Chapter 4, a group of committed citizens started a petition campaign against *Il legittimo impedimento,* an Act of Parliament introduced to prevent a trial against Prime Minister Silvio Berlusconi's not always transparent business interests. In June 2011, 95 per cent of the voters – on a 57 per cent turnout – abrogated the law. Often, Italian voters do not bother and elect to stay at home. Not this time. After years of absurdly sordid revelations about the prime minister's *Bonga-Bonga* parties, the Italian voters sent a clear message via referendum. A few months later, *Il Cavaliere* (as the diminutive Italian tycoon and politician calls himself) was forced out of office. The referendum was, as the left-leaning newspaper *La Repubblica* concluded, 'proof that [Italian] democracy worked' (Rosso 2011: A3).

Britain is not, and will never be, Italy. Political institutions cannot be transplanted as if they were garden herbs. But political institutions and practices can provide inspirations as well as warnings. This short book has merely presented the briefest of historical outlines of how referendums have been used in Britain and abroad. In doing so it has implicitly presented some of the arguments for and against this institution. It is now up to the reader to decide how we can improve upon a political institution that is here to stay; inaction is not an option.

Further reading

Altman, D. (2011) *Direct Democracy Worldwide*. Cambridge, Cambridge University Press.

Atikcan, E.Ö. (2015) *Framing the European Union: The Power of Political Arguments in Shaping European Integration*. Cambridge, Cambridge University Press.

Bogdanor, V. (1981) *The People and the Party System: The Referendum and Electoral Reform in British Politics*. Cambridge, Cambridge University Press

Bowler, S., Donovan, T. and Tolbert, C.J. (1998) *Citizens as Legislators: Direct Democracy in the United States*. Columbus, Ohio State University Press.

LeDuc, L. (2003) *The Politics of Direct Democracy: Referendums in Global Perspective*. Toronto, Broadview Press.

Magleby, D.B. (1984) *Direct Legislation: Voting on Ballot Propositions in the United States*. Baltimore, Johns Hopkins University Press.

Matsusaka, J.G. (2008) *For the Many or the Few: The Initiative, Public Policy, and American Democracy*. Chicago, University of Chicago Press.

Mendez, F., Mendez, M. and Triga, V. (2014) *Referendums and the European Union: A Comparative Inquiry*. Cambridge, Cambridge University Press.

Qvortrup, M. (2005) *A Comparative Study of Referendums: Government by the People*. Manchester, Manchester University Press.

Qvortrup, M. (2017) *Direct Democracy: A Comparative Study of the*

Theory and Practice of Government by the People. Manchester, Manchester University Press.

Ruth, S.P., Welp, Y. and Whitehead, L. (2017) *Direct Democracy in the Twenty-first Century*. Colchester, ECPR Press.

Setälä, M. and Schiller, T. (eds) (2009) *Referendums and Representative Democracy: Responsiveness, Accountability and Deliberation*. London, Routledge.

Tierney, S. (2012) *Constitutional Referendums: The Theory and Practice of Republican Deliberation*. Oxford, Oxford University Press.

References

Almond, G.A., Dalton, R.J., Powell, G.B. and Strøm, K. (2006) *Comparative Politics Today: A World View.* New York, Pearson Longman.

Altman, D. (2011) *Direct Democracy Worldwide.* Cambridge, Cambridge University Press.

Archives Parlementaires (1875) 1 Series, vol. 25. Paris, P. Dupont.

Arendt, Hannah (1968) *Between Past and Future.* New York, Penguin.

Aristotle (2006) *Art of Rhetoric,* translated by J.H. Freese, Cambridge, MA, Harvard University Press, Loeb Classical Library.

Atikcan, E.Ö. (2015) *Framing the European Union: The Power of Political Arguments in Shaping European Integration.* Cambridge, Cambridge University Press.

Balsom, Denis (1996) 'The United Kingdom: Constitutional Pragmatism and the Adoption of the Referendum', in Michael Gallagher and Pier Vincenzo Uleri (eds), *The Referendum Experience in Europe.* London, Macmillan.

BBC (2012) 'MP Dorries Calls PM and Chancellor "Arrogant Posh Boys"', *Today,* 23 April. www.bbc.co.uk/news/uk-politics-17815769 (accessed 1 August 2017).

BBC (2014) 'Scottish Independence: Prof Patrick Dunleavy Says Treasury Claims "Ludicrous"', *Today,* 28 May. www.bbc.co.uk/news/uk-scotland-scotland-politics-27611563 (accessed 1 August 2017).

Berbera, A. and Morrone, A. (2003) *La Repubblica dei referendum:* Bologna: Il Mulino.

Berelson, B. (1954) *Voting: A Study of Opinion Formation in a Presidential Campaign*. Chicago, University of Chicago Press.

Bernard, Laurent (2012) *Campaign Strategy in Direct Democracy*. Basingstoke, Palgrave.

Bodin, Jean (1986) [1579] *Les six livres de la République*. Lyon: De L'Imprimérie de Jean de Tournes.

Bogdanor, V.B. (1981a) *The People and the Party System: The Referendum and Electoral Reform in British Politics*. Cambridge, Cambridge University Press.

Bogdanor V.B. (1981b) 'Referendums and Separatism II', in Austin Ranney (ed.), *The Referendum Device*. Washington, American Enterprise Institute.

Buckley, Stephen (2006) *The Prime Minister and Cabinet*. Edinburgh, Edinburgh University Press.

Bullock, I. and Reynolds, S. (1987) 'How British and French Socialists Viewed the Referendum', *History Workshop*, 24 (autumn), 62–81.

Butler, D. and Butler, G. (1994) *British Political Facts 1900–1994*, London, Macmillan.

Butler, David and Kavanagh, Dennis (1974) *The British General Election of February 1974*. London, Macmillan.

Butler, David and Kitzinger, Uwe W. (1976) *The 1975 Referendum*. London, Macmillan.

Cairney, P. (2015) 'The Scottish Independence Referendum: What Are the Implications of a No Vote?', *The Political Quarterly*, 86(2), 186–91.

Campbell, A., Converse, P.E., Miller, W.E. and Stokes, D.E. (1980) [1961] *The American Voter*. Chicago, University of Chicago Press.

Cavour, Camillo di (1883) *Lettere edite ed inedite di Camillo Cavour*, ed. Luigi Chiala. Turin, Roux.

Churchill, Winston (1946) 'Address Given by Winston Churchill (Zurich, 19 September 1946', transcript. Quoted in www.Europe.eu: http://europa.eu/about-eu/eu-history/founding-fathers/pdf/winston_churchill_en.pdf (accessed 1 August 2017).

Condorcet, Marie Jean (1847) *Sur la Necessité de faire Ratifier la Constitution par les Citoyens*. Paris, Arago.

Daily Express, (2016) 'Brexit Shock – France "Overtakes UK as World's Fifth Largest Economy" after Pound Plunges', 24 June. www.express.co.uk/finance/city/683003/Brexit-shock-France-overtakes-UK-worlds-fifth-largest-economy-pound-plunges (accessed 25 June 2016).

The Daily Telegraph (2016) 'Nigel Farage: £350 Million Pledge to Fund the NHS Was "a mistake"', 24 June.

Dassonneville, Ruth (2012) 'Electoral Volatility, Political Sophistication, Trust and Efficacy', *Acta Politica*, 47 (January): 18–41.

de Gaulle, Charles (1971) *Memoirs of Hope*. London, Weidenfeld and Nicolson.

de Klerk, Frederik W. (1999) *The Last Trek: A New Beginning: The Autobiography*. London, Macmillan.

Della Porta, D. (2006) *Social Movements, Political Violence, and the State: A Comparative Analysis of Italy and Germany*. Cambridge, Cambridge University Press.

Diamond, Larry, (2015) 'Facing up to the Democratic Recession', in Larry Diamond and Marc F. Plattner (eds), *Democracy in Decline*. Baltimore, Johns Hopkins University Press, pp. 98–118.

Dicey, A.V. (1890) 'Ought the Referendum to Be Introduced into England?', *Contemporary Review*, pp. 500–10.

Dicey, A.V. (1911) *A Leap in the Dark*, London, John Murray.

Dicey, A.V. (1981) [1915] *An Introduction to the Study of the Law of the Constitution*. Indianapolis, Liberty Fund.

Dilnot, Sir Andrew (2016) in *UK Statistics Authority*, 11 May. www.statisticsauthority.gov.uk/news/uk-statistics-authority-statement-on-the-use-of-official-statistics-on-contributions-to-the-european-union/ (accessed 12 June 2016).

Dryden, John (2010) [1681] *Absalom and Achitophel*. Helena, MT, Kessinger Publishing.

The Economist (2016) 'Next Stop Brexit!', 11 March.

Erasmus, Desiderius (1907) [1517] *Erasmus Against War*, ed. J.W. Mackail. Boston, Merrymount Press.

Farley, Lawrence T. (1986) *Plebiscites and Sovereignty: The Crisis of Political Legitimacy*. Boulder, Westview Press.

Frey, B and Stuzer, A. (2000) 'Happiness, the Economy and Institutions', *The Economic Journal*, 110(4): 918–38.

Geertz, Clifford (1973) *The Interpretation of Cultures: Selected Essays*. New York, Basic Books.

Glencross, A. (2016) *Why the UK Voted for Brexit: David Cameron's Great Miscalculation*. London, Palgrave, Pivot.

Goebbels, J. (1934) SA-Appell, [Speech to the SA] Berlin, 25 August 1934. Hamburg, Hoffmann und Campe Verlag.

Goodhart, Philip (1971) *Referendum*. London, Tom Stacey.

Griffiths, M. (2003) 'Self-Determination, International Society and World Order', *Macquarie Law Journal*, 3(1): 29–49.

Grotius, Hugo (2005) [1625] *The Rights of War and Peace*, ed. K. Haakonsen. Indianapolis, Liberty Fund.

The Guardian (2016) 'John Major: EU Leave Campaign at Risk of "Divisive" Immigration Stance', 12 May. www.theguardian.com/politics/2016/may/12/john-major-eu-leave-campaigners-risk-turning-into-ukip (accessed 16 March 2017).

The Guardian (2016) 'Queen and Brexit Row: Gove Refuses to Rule out Being Sun's Source', 12 March. www.theguardian.com/politics/2016/mar/12/queen-and-brexit-row-gove-refuses-to-rule-out-being-suns-source (accessed 5 April 2017).

Guillaume-Hofnung, M. (1987) *Le referendum* Paris, PUF.

Hansen, M.H. (1991) *The Athenian Democracy in the Age of Demosthenes: Structure, Principles, and Ideology*. Norman, University of Oklahoma Press.

Hayward, J.E.S. (1969) 'Presidential Suicide by Plebiscite: De Gaulle's Exit, April 1969', *Parliamentary Affairs*, 22(2): 289–319.

Hennessy, Patrick (2016) 'Let's Quit EU Say 46 Per Cent of Voters in Poll', *The Daily Telegraph*, 18 May. www.telegraph.co.uk/news/politics/10066273/Lets-quit-EU-say-46-per-cent-of-voters-in-poll.html (accessed 16 March 2017).

Hobhouse, L.T. (1994) [1911] *Liberalism and Other Writings.* Cambridge, Cambridge University Press.

Hobson, J.A. (1909) *The Crisis of Liberalism: New Issues of Democracy.* London, P.S. King & Sons.

Hodges, Dan (2011) 'No We Can', *New Statesman*, 16 May: 37.

Holmberg, Sören (2000) 'Issue Agreement', in P. Eliasson and K. Heidar (eds), *Beyond Westminster and Congress: The Nordic Experience.* Columbus, University of Ohio State University Press, pp. 155–80.

House of Commons (2016) *The Economic and Financial Costs and Benefits of the UK's EU membership*, House of Commons, HC-122, 26 May.

Huntington, S.P. (1975) 'The Democratic Distemper', *The Public Interest*, 41: 9–38.

'Iain Duncan Smith Resignation Letter' (2016) BBC, *Today*, 18 March. www.bbc.co.uk/news/uk-politics-35848891 (accessed 1 August 2017).

The Independent (2016) 'EU Referendum: Boris Johnson Accused of "Dishonest Gymnastics" over TTIP U-turn', 15 May. www.independent.co.uk/news/uk/politics/eu-referendum-boris-johnson-accused-of-dishonest-gymnastics-over-ttip-u-turn-a7030981.html (accessed 11 April 2017).

Kautsky, Karl (1893) 'Die direkte Gesetzgebung durch das Volk und der Klassenkampf', *Die Neue Zeit*, 11(2): 516–27.

Kautsky, Karl (1911) *Parlamentarismus und Demokratie.* Stuttgart, J.H.W. Dietz.

Keegan, William (2016) 'What Whitehall Farce', *The Observer*, 24 July: A43.

Knock, K. (2006) 'The North East Referendum: Lessons Learnt?', *Parliamentary Affairs*, 59(4): 682–93.

The Labour Party (1972) *Report of the Seventy-first Annual Party Conference of the Labour Party Blackpool 1972.* London, The Labour Party.

Lasch, C. (1996) *The Revolt of the Elites and the Betrayal of Democracy.* New York, W.W. Norton & Company.

Leleu, Claude (1976) 'The French Referendum of April 23, 1972', *European Journal of Political Research*, 4(1): 25–46.

Lenin V.I. (1948) *Imperialism, the Highest Stage of Capitalism.* London, Lawrence and Wishart.

Levitsky, Steven and Way, Lucan (2002) 'The Rise of Competitive Authoritarianism', *Journal of Democracy*, 13(2): 51–65.

Levitsky, Steven and Way, Lucan (2010) *Competitive Authoritarianism: Hybrid Regimes after the Cold War.* Cambridge, Cambridge University Press.

Linz, Juan J. (2000) *Totalitarian and Authoritarian Regimes.* Boulder, Lynne Rienner Publishers.

Loizides, Neophytos (2016) *Designing Peace: Cyprus and Institutional Innovations in Divided Societies.* Philadelphia, University of Pennsylvania Press.

MacDonald, R. (1911) *The Socialist Movement.* London, Holt and Company.

Machiavelli, N (1848) *Discorsi sopra la prima deca di Tito Livio di Niccolò Machiavelli.* Florence, Felice Le Monnier.

Mail Online (2016) 'Farage Thinks Remain Has Carried Referendum as Votes Are Counted', 23 June. www.dailymail.co.uk/wires/pa/article-3655449/Voters-set-to-polls-EU-referendum-day.html (last accessed 1 August 2017).

Maine, Henry S. (1976) [1885] *Popular Government.* Indianapolis, Liberty Fund.

Martens, G.F. von (1801) *Recueil de Principaux traits d'alliance de paix.* Göttingen, J.C. Dieterich.

Marx, Karl (2000) 'Critique of the Gotha Programme', ed. David McLellan, in *Karl Marx: Selected Writings. Second Edition.* Oxford, Oxford University Press, pp. 610–16.

Matsusaka, John G. (1992) 'Economics of Direct Legislation', *The Quarterly Journal of Economics*, 107 (March): 541–7.

McAllister, L. and Cole, M. (2012) 'The 2011 Welsh General Election: An Analysis of the Latest Staging Post in the Maturing of Welsh Politics', *Parliamentary Affairs*, 67(1): 172–90.

Munro, William (1912) *The Initiative, the Referendum and the Recall*. New York, D. Appleton.

Murray, B.K. (1973) 'The Politics of the People's Budget', *The Historical Journal*, 16(3): 555–70.

New York Times (1921) 'French Try to Stop Tyrol Plebiscite: Vote on Annexation to Germany Set for April 24 Strongly Opposed by Paris', 11 April: A6.

No to AV (2011) 'Keep One Person One Vote: Vote No in the Referendum on 5 May', London, No Campaign Ltd.

Noble, L.G. (1976) 'Philippines 1975: Consolidating the Regime', *Asian Survey*, 16 (June): 178–85.

Office of Budget Responsibility (2016) *Economic and Fiscal Outlook – March 2016*. London, TSO.

Orwell, George (2014) 'The Lion and the Unicorn', in *Essays*. London, Penguin, pp. 138–87.

Pieth, F. (1958) 'Das altbündnerische Referendum' *Bündner Monatsblatt: Zeitschrift für Geschichte, Landes- und Volkskunde*, 5 (May): 137–53.

Pugh, M. (2000) *The March of the Women: A Revisionist Analysis of the Campaign for Women's Suffrage, 1866–1914*. Oxford, Oxford University Press.

Qvortrup, M. (2012) 'Voting on Electoral Reform: A Comparative Perspective on the Alternative Vote Referendum in the United Kingdom', *The Political Quarterly*, 83(1): 108–16.

Qvortrup, M. (ed.) (2014) *Referendums Around the World: The Continued Growth of Direct Democracy*. London, Palgrave Macmillan.

Qvortrup, M. (2016) 'Referendums on Membership and European Integration 1972–2015', *The Political Quarterly*, 87(1): 61–8.

Qvortrup, M. (2017) *Direct Democracy: A Comparative Study of the Theory and Practice of Government by the People*. Manchester, Manchester University Press.

Rokkan, Stein and Lipset, Seymour M. (1967) 'Cleavage Structures, Party Systems, and Voter Alignments', in Stein Rokkan and Seymour M. Lipset (eds), *Party Systems and Voter*

Alignments: Cross-National Perspectives. New York, The Free Press.

Rosso, U. (2011) 'Il Quirinale Soddisfatto una prova di democrazia', *La Repubblica*, 14 June, A3.

Särlvik, B., Crewe, I., Alt, J. and Fox, A. (1976) 'Britain's Membership of the EEC: A Profile of Electoral Opinions in the Spring of 1974 – with a Postscript on the Referendum', *European Journal of Political Research*, 4(1): 83–113.

Schama, Simon (2016) 'Let Us Write Our Own History to Remain a Beacon of Tolerance', *Financial Times*, 18 June, A13.

Schiller, Theo (ed.) (2011) *Local Direct Democracy in Europe.* Wiesbaden, VS-Verlag.

Schmitt, C. (1988) *The Crisis of Parliamentary Democracy*, translated by Ellen Kennedy. Cambridge, MA, MIT Press.

Schneider, Lisa C. (2011) 'Violence and State Repression', *Swiss Political Science Review*, 17 (December): 480–4.

Seldon, Anthony and Snowdon, Peter (2015) *Cameron at 10.* Glasgow, William Collins.

Serdült, U. (2017) 'Switzerland', in M. Qvortrup (ed.), *Referendums around the World.* London, Palgrave Macmillan, pp. 47–112.

Sharp, C. (1911) *The Case Against the Referendum.* London, Fabian Tract no.155.

Solière, Eugène (1901) *Le Plébiscite dans l'annexion. Étude historique et critique de droit des gens.* Paris, L. Boyer.

Steinmo, Sven (2008) *Structuring Politics: Historical Institutionalism in Comparative Analysis.* Cambridge, Cambridge University Press.

Stevens, Nick (2010) 'A Passion for Politics', in The Economic and Social Research Council, *Britain in 2011.* London, ESRC, pp. 50–1.

Stone, Jon (2016) 'EU "in" Campaign Chief Lord Rose Says His Side Will Win by "a substantial margin"', *The Independent*, 5 February. www.independent.co.uk/news/uk/politics/eu-in-campaign-chief-lord-rose-says-his-side-will-win-by-a-substantial-margin-a6854951.html (last accessed 1 August 2017).

The Sun (2016) 'Remain Shame', (editorial), 20 June: A10.

Tacitus (1970) *The Agricola and Germania*. London, Penguin.

Tierney, S. (2012) *Constitutional Referendums: The Theory and Practice of Republican Deliberation*. Oxford, Oxford University Press.

Tocqueville, Alexis de (1961) *Democracy in America. Vol. I*. New York, Vintage.

Topaloff, L. (2017) 'Elite Strategy or Populist Weapon?', *Journal of Democracy*, 28(3): 127–40.

Tuck, Richard (2016) *The Sleeping Sovereign: The Invention of Modern Democracy*. Cambridge, Cambridge University Press.

Uleri, Pier V. (2002) 'On Referendum Voting in Italy: YES, NO or Non–vote? How Italian Parties Learned to Control Referendums', *European Journal of Political Research*, 41 (October2): 863–83.

Vattel, E. (1758) *Le droit des gens: ou, Principes de la loi naturelle, appliqués à la conduite & aux affaires des nations & des souverains* (Vol. 1). Paris, Aux depens de la Compagnie.

Wambaugh, S. (1933) *Plebiscites since the World War: With a Collection of Official Documents* (Vol. 1). New York, Carnegie Endowment for International Peace.

Weber, Max (1958) 'Deutschlands künftige Staatsform', in *Gesammelte Politische Schriften,* 2nd expanded edition, ed. Johannes Winckelmann. Tübingen, J.C.B. Mohr (Paul Siebeck), pp. 448–83.

Weitz, E.D. (2008) 'From the Vienna to the Paris System: International Politics and the Entangled Histories of Human Rights, Forced Deportations, and Civilizing Missions', *The American Historical Review*, 113(5): 1313–43.

Wilson, Harold (1974) *Let Us Work Together – Labour's Way out of the Crisis*. London: The Labour Party. http://www.politics-resources.net/area/uk/man/lab74feb.htm (accessed 1 August 2017).

Wittgenstein, Ludwig (1953) *Philosophical Investigations*. Oxford, Blackwell.

Index